The Jungle Beat

Fighting Terrorists in Malaya

Roy Follows

Publisher TravellersEye
Editor Dan Hiscocks

The Jungle Beat

2nd Edition

Published by TravellersEye Ltd, October 1999

Head Office:

30 St Mary's Street

Bridgnorth

Shropshire

WV16 4DW

tel: (0044) 1746 766447

fax: (0044) 1746 766665

website:www.travellerseye.com

email: books@travellerseye.com

Set in Times,

ISBN: 0953057577

Printed and bound in Great Britain by Creative Print & Design Group. 1st Edition published by Blandford, Cassell, 1990. Co-author Hugh Popham.

contents

list of abbreviations

ASAL	Communist organisation which controlled the aborigines. From *asal*, Malay for 'origin'; hence *orang asal,* 'original person', i.e.aborigine.
ASP	Assistant Superintendent of Police
BCM	Branch Committee Member
CEP	Captured Enemy Personnel
CID	Criminal Investigation Department
CO	Commanding Officer
CT	Communist Terrorist
DCM	District Committee Member (of the Communist Party)
DZ	Dropping Zone (for airborne supplies)
HQ	Headquarters
KL	Kuala Lumpur
LZ	Landing Zone
MCP	Malayan Communist Party
MIO	Military Intelligence Officer
MP	Military Police
MPAJA	Malayan Peoples' Anti-Japanese Army
MR	Map reference
MRLA	Malayan Races' Liberation Army
NJP	North Johore Politburo
OC	Officer Commanding
PAG	Police Aboriginal Guard
PC	Police Constable
PFF	Police Field Force
REME	Royal Electrical and Mechanical Engineers
RV	Rendezvous
SB	Special Branch
SEP	Surrendered Enemy Personnel
SF	Security Forces
SITREP	Situation Report
SOVF	Special Operations Volunteer Force
W/Op	Wireless Operator

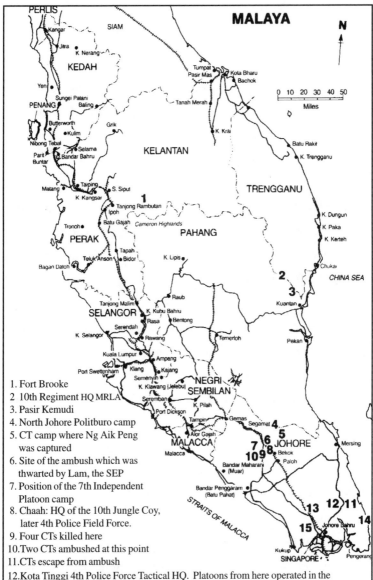

1. Fort Brooke
2. 10th Regiment HQ MRLA
3. Pasir Kemudi
4. North Johore Politburo camp
5. CT camp where Ng Aik Peng was captured
6. Site of the ambush which was thwarted by Lam, the SEP
7. Position of the 7th Independent Platoon camp
8. Chaah: HQ of the 10th Jungle Coy, later 4th Police Field Force.
9. Four CTs killed here
10. Two CTs ambushed at this point
11. CTs escape from ambush
12. Kota Tinggi 4th Police Force Tactical HQ. Platoons from here operated in the Pengerang area and other southern and central areas of Johore.
13. Kulai HQ, 4th Police Field Force. They covered operations anywhere in Johore and sometimes outside the State
14. The CT camp where I left the doctored ammunition
15. Covert operations with the SOVF which resulted in the capture of CTs

foreword

When I picked up Roy Follows' book, I was in some doubt as to whether there are people interested in a forgotten war; a war, in fact, that never was. But then, when I started reading I realised this wasn't an ordinary book of war memoirs. This is a real book. It's a book that graphically brings back the sweat and the fear of the cloying, claustrophobic jungle at its most un-neutral; the perpetual damp from head to toe, the cold bitter first light struggling into yesterday's mud encrusted and sweat soaked uniform and reluctantly stuffing out of sight the almost dry kit in which one had slept a fitful half awake night, waiting for the explosion of an enemy charge. Of week after week of trudging through stinking swamp, struggling from root to root of mangrove swamps, and then the all pervading fear when a sign, no more than a scuffed foot print or a cut twig, showed that you were either in the middle of an ambush and were about to be killed or you were near a heavily armed enemy camp. And all this deep in the jungle, miles from civilisation. It's all here, and if you haven't felt fear before, you will now as you go with Roy Follows on a six year battle with Chinese Communists.

But Roy Follows had some special attributes; he was an exceptionally brave man; he had an enormous sense of humour and a great wit, and he had that indefinable something that made him a born leader. And he was lucky. He was lucky to have Fred Milner MC as his commanding officer who recognised these qualities and gave him virtual carte blanche to get on with the job of hunting down terrorists. Shorn of rules and regulations and being able to do things his way was exactly Roy's cup of tea. Within a very short time he was speaking fluent Malay and had won the respect, loyalty, and - indeed a rare distinction – the devotion for a European officer of his Malay jungle fighters. But Roy Follows wouldn't have considered popularity let alone affection from his men as in any way necessary to his mission. He failed to understand the affection behind it when his platoon sergeant, Shaffie, once barged him aside when he was about to charge through a one-man-at-a-time gap into a heavily defended enemy camp and rushed in before him. Shaffie later explained that he didn't much fancy the shame and humiliation of returning to camp with a dead Leptenen Pollo; the men would cut his throat, so better he take the first burst of Bren than *Tuan*!

Follows and Shaffie made an extraordinary lethal team of jungle fighters. They respected and admired each other; two men different in every possible respect – Roy over six feet tall and weighing about as much as half a dozen new laid eggs looked like a stick insect, whereas Shaffie was stockily built, round faced and wouldn't have reached five feet standing on tiptoe – yet they possessed the same sense of humour and dedication, and were very close friends. They gave no quarter in the jungle. And quarter was one thing they didn't expect and knew they wouldn't have got it. It was a hard and bitter war.

Roy Follows made the perfect jungle fighter. He had no pretensions; he didn't command – he led, and he led from the front;

he rarely raised his voice yet he achieved more from his men with just a look, a smile, or a grimace than others managed with apoplexy in trying to get the thing right.

This book in its earlier edition is considered essential reading for officers in jungle appointments. In Brunei it is used as a *modus operandi*, and young officers with the mention of 'mosquito repellent' anywhere on their posting order would be well advised to invest in *The Jungle Beat*, read it, and thank themselves lucky that wherever they serve it's 1999 and not the 1950's. To readers for whom all this is new ground, the book at the very least presents a dramatic close-up of an exciting but almost-forgotten piece of our history at the sunset of the Empire.

It delivers to the curious and to the adventurous of all generations what used to be called a rattling good yarn. It tells it exactly how it was. It is a bit grisly in places, and definitely not for the squeamish. But neither is war.

George Brown, 1999.

Bestselling author of *The Double Tenth* and *Sacrifice*.

one

a cushy job?

The small village police post of Pasir Kemudi, midway between Kuantan and Sungei Lembing, was a wooden building encased in sandbags. My quarters consisted of a Malay shack, built on stilts. The police officer I took over from had been relieved of his duties because of a nervous breakdown. The one narrow dirt road that led to Kuantan twisted and turned through the jungle, and had often been ambushed; many Malay police had been killed on it. Whenever I used it, I opened fire with the bren-gun into any likely ambush position, just in case. I was twenty-three, very green, and very scared.

At night, in my atap hut, I used to jam the door with furniture, and put the bren-gun on the table at the ready. When I lit the paraffin lamp to read, I squatted on the floor out of sight, so as not to present a sitting target. The area was under the control of the Communist 10th Regiment; this, unlike the other Communist formations throughout Malaya (which were largely recruited from the Chinese), was made up mainly of Malays. As far as I was concerned in those early days, there could well have been a terrorist behind every tree.

I had to turn native overnight. I washed in the river alongside the villagers and learnt to adapt my diet to one of rice with everything. I could not speak the language but could just about make myself understood - or more often misunderstood.

While I was in Pasir Kemudi I served my apprenticeship in jungle-craft. Most days I would take a small patrol out, just to get the feel of the terrain: almost at once I found I was attracted by the jungle; something seemed to hold me fast to it. I couldn't, I still can't, fully describe the fascination it exerted on me, but it was very real. This was in spite of the fact that often, after a number of hours patrolling, my navigation came unstuck. One problem was that I always thought I had walked further than I actually had. It takes a long time to appreciate just how slow one's progress through heavy rain forest can be - at worst, perhaps only half a dozen miles in a day. I shall never forget the first night I spent in the jungle. I had no proper kit and only a small groundsheet to lie on. I tried to make some sort of cover out of palm fronds, but my work proved absolutely useless and when it rained, just after dark, my thick brown army blanket and everything else became sodden within minutes. I sat up, wet and shivering, and spent a miserable night being attacked by mosquitoes.

It was on one of these apprentice patrols that I came across my first Communist camp. The occupants, about ten of them, happened to be away, which was undoubtedly lucky for me. I had failed to notice the give-away signs that we were approaching a camp; and the language problem prevented the few men who were with me from voicing their suspicions. As a result, I found myself standing inside the Communist stronghold before I realised it. Inside the shelters we found some haversacks, which we removed (we heard later that they contained important documents). While I was rummaging through one of them, I came across a small tin containing some sort of powder. Before any of the men could stop me, I had tipped it out on the ground - how was I to know that it was opium!.

On another occasion, out on a five-day patrol, I blundered into a huge camp not far from the Sungei Reman. It had accommodation for at least one hundred and must have been evacuated only a few hours before we arrived. Little did I realise, as we took refuge for the night in a cave on the side of a huge limestone outcrop, with insect-infested ground to lie on and bats flying around our heads, how lucky we had been. When I eventually got the news of the camp back to Kuantan police headquarters, they sent for me straight away and interrogated me closely. I told them about the number of *bashas*, the parade ground and all the rest of it and they listened in amazement. Apparently, I had stumbled across the HQ of the 10th Regiment, which the Gurkhas has vainly spent weeks searching for. If the camp had been occupied, my small ill-equipped patrol would have been wiped out to a man!

In retrospect, I would say it was sheer folly to send untrained young men like me into the jungle. Still, with each patrol my jungle-craft and navigation skills improved, as did my knowledge of the Malay language. There would be no more of those embarrassing incidents like the time when I tried to halt the patrol in order to relieve myself, and they obediently followed me. After almost eight months, I felt I had acquired the necessary skills, and I applied for a transfer to a jungle company as a platoon commander. This was where the real war against the Communists was being fought.

When I first joined the Malayan Police in May 1952, I had had absolutely no experience of warfare, let alone the very specialised kind of warfare that was being waged aginst the terrorists of the Malayan Communist Party, the MCP.

Born in North Staffordshire, I left school at fourteen and was apprenticed as a fitter at the locomotive works at Crewe. Although I enjoyed the work, I had a yearning for adventure and wild country, especially jungle; and not realising that that was the only thing I shouldn't find there, I applied to join the Palestine Police. This, of course, was before the creation of the State of Israel, and the job was to keep the peace between the Palestinians and Israeli terrorist organisations like Ergun Zwer Leumi - a situation rather like the present one in Ulster. However, I was rejected - on the grounds that I wasn't heavy enough!

After National Service, working on plant and equipment with the REME entirely in the UK, I found my longing to travel was as strong as ever; and so, instead of going back to the engine-shops, I went to sea as a junior engineer with Ellerman Lines. For two years the *City of Poona* took me all over the world; but then I was sent to engineering college in Liverpool. Three months of that was quite enough, and when I saw an advertisement for vacancies in the Malayan Police I applied, and - having put on some weight - was accepted. With three other 'new boys' - Alec Wilmott, an artist, Joe O'Brian, an ex-para, and Paul Bonney, an RAF pilot (but he didn't take to it and soon opted out) - I flew out to Singapore in a Constellation in May 1952.

In the naval barracks there, we kicked our heels for a fortnight and then were sent to Tanjong Kling on the Malacca coast before going off to join a unit. While we were there we never went into the jungle, were given no training and never even fired a weapon. That's what I meant when I said that on my first posting to Kuantan, Pahang, I was green. In fact, because of my sea background, the first posting I was offered when I arrived in Malaya was with the Marine Police on Penang Island. When I turned it down, the jaw of the elderly police superintendent who was interviewing me dropped in sheer disbelief. He leant back in his chair, to get the full effect of the slowly turning fan on the ceiling above his head, and stared at me.

'You mean you do not want the Penang posting?'

'That is correct, Sir,' I said.

'I can't believe it, most people would do anything to get it. Anything. With your experience, ideal.....why won't you take it?'

'Well, Sir, I joined the Malay Police to fight the Communists, not mess about in little boats.'

'I see, want excitement, adventure, is that it?'

'Yes, Sir.'

'You remind me of myself when I was a young man,' he said, and proceeded to give me his military and police autobiography. Eventually he said, 'Leave it with me.' I saluted and left.

Several hours later he sent for me again.

'I've been on to Kuala Lumpur. They've granted your request. They are posting you to Kuantan, Pahang on the east coast.'

'Thank you, Sir.' I hesitated. 'What's it like there Sir?'

'Grim. Bloody grim, Follows. Communists are running the place...do as they please.' He shook his head, but whether it was because of the Communists, or me, I didn't know. After a pause, he went on: 'Your two years' National Service won't have prepared you for this show. It's a dirty, dangerous war; ask anyone who was here in 1942, '43 or '44, they'll tell you.'

'Yes Sir,' I said. To me, even the words 'Pahang Kuantan' had a mysterious ring to them. 'When do I leave?'

'You'll fly up in four days' time. Good luck Follows.' He stood up and shook me by the hand, 'You'll need it.'

How right he was!

Here I should perhaps say something about why we were involved in this conflict at all. Although the Malayan Communist Party (MCP) dates back to 1922, only after World War 2 did it move into action and try to take over the country. During the Japanese occupation it was the Communists, through the guerrilla groups of their Malayan Peoples' Anti-Japanese Army, the MPAJA, who formed the most effective opposition to the occupying troops. Ironically, the members of the MPAJA were provided with arms by the British; and, although they were supposed to hand them in after the Japanese surrender, most of them were hidden for future use - against us. Their campaign to take over the country, backed by both Moscow and China (the majority of their members were Chinese), began immediately with attempts to infiltrate and manipulate the emerging trade unions first in Singapore, then on the mainland of Malaya, but they soon turned to open violence. In June 1948, three European planters were murdered by a Chinese Communist gang near Ipoh and a State of Emergency was declared. Their attempt, soon afterwards, to create a Communist-controlled 'Liberated Area' around Kota Bharu, on the north-east coast, was so soundly defeated, however, that they were forced to retreat into the jungle. There, through an unpleasant mixture of propaganda and terror, they attempted to organise enough popular support to challenge, and eventually overthrow, the Government. Because, for nearly 80 years, Malaya - or the Federated Malay States, as it was known - had been under British protection, and because, with its valuable assets of Singapore as a base, and rubber and tin from its estates and mines, it was a jewel in the Imperial Crown, and because the West felt the importance of resisting Communism wherever it surfaced, the British were bound to become involved.

There were two main forces fighting the CTs; one was the army and the other was the Malayan Police. Army units, notably the Gurkhas, but also The Fijians, King's African Rifles, Sarawak Rangers, and a number of regular battalions from Britain fought there, many of the last including soldiers doing their National Service. The Police Field Force, the operational arm of the Malayan Police - to which I belonged - was composed largely of Malays, with mainly British officers, though while I was there more and more Malays were being commissioned.

Vernon Bartlett, writing in 1953[1] - the year I went to Yong Peng - had this to say:

' the CTs are most definitely on the defensive; they, more often than the police or the soldiers, are the victims of ambushes

....Patrols by the Police Field Force or the army are increasingly effective, but a man does an average of seven hundred hours 'jungle-bashing' before he kills a Communist'.

This story deals, as it must, with the highlights of my five and a half years in the jungle. The reader must use his imagination to fill in the hundreds of hours of 'jungle-bashing' that came between the events I describe. Soldiering there, as always everywhere, is ninety-nine per cent boredom and one per cent excitement.

In due course I was informed that my request for a posting had been granted and I was told to report to Cha'ah in North Johore.

two

from a view to kill

The Labis-Yong Peng area of North Johore was overrun with Communist terrorists (CTs); Cha'ah, to which I had been posted, was the centre of their activities. The 10th Police Jungle Coy, in which I was now a platoon commander, was one of the units specialising in deep jungle penetration, and we were properly equipped for our role of seeking out and destroying Communist hide-outs. Where, earlier, the CTs had been safe in their lairs to which, having attacked a police station or ambushed a Security Forces (SF) patrol, they could retreat unmolested, this was no longer the case. Companies like the 10th Police could stay in the jungle for weeks, supplied by air, and could take the battle into the heart of the enemy's country. I was to be with this company for twenty one months.

Our main opponents at Cha'ah were the 7th CT Platoon under its Political Commissar, Goh Peng Tuan, and the numerous Communist cells in the local villages. Goh Peng's gang were killers and absolutely ruthless. Several times we were ordered out to bring back their victims; normally it would be one of the rubber estate workers, men whose job is to tap the latex from the rubber trees. More often than not they had been horribly tortured before being murdered. The usual reason behind the killings was the refusal of the villagers to pay the monthly subscription demanded by the

Communists. When, on one of these grim sorties, I found that the man concerned had been mutilated and killed in the presence of his wife and son, I swore that, one day, I would make the CTs pay for their revolting crimes.

Several times during those weeks I found camps which had been abandoned by the 7th Platoon, so it appeared that they were keeping on the move in order to give us the slip. Our first real chance went awry by a stroke of misfortune. I had disguised three or four of the Chinese members of my platoon as CTs, and with them as the lure, I had laid a trap which should have bagged the entire outfit. What's more, they very nearly walked straight into it. Unfortunately a party of rubber tappers saw us and gave the terrorists warning of our presence. But there was always a next time. As it happened, the District Committee Member's mother and younger brother lived in the village, and I knew them both by sight. One day the mother was caught smuggling dog flesh (the Chinese believe it cures malaria) out of the village, which meant that the District Committee Member was ill in his jungle camp. I knew this from an informer of mine, so I saw the brother and asked him why they had been meeting him, but he feigned innocence.

One of our weapons against the CTs was a leaflet calling on them to give themselves up. If they did, and behaved themselves, their crimes would be overlooked and they would be handsomely treated. If they did not, they could be sure their days were numbered. Literally thousands of these sheets were distributed, the bulk of them from the air, and they had some effect, the more so as the Security Forces started to get the upper hand. I now gave one to the brother.

'Next time you see the District Committee Member,' I said, 'give him this. Tell him that if he doesn't come out of the jungle and give himself up, I shall kill him.'

Nothing happened. Then, several days later, Police Lieutenant George Brown and I, with a small party, were making our way back towards the main trunk road after a short patrol, to meet the transport to take us back to camp. My diary describes what happened next:

august 1953

Walking through an oil palm estate about 20 yards from the road, saw a group of armed figures in the lalang on the opposite side to us. They were also walking towards the road, but seemed unaware of our presence. Only about 50 yards separated us. I knew it must be the district committee member and his men.

We dropped to the ground and crawled forward until we reached the road. As we jumped to our feet the leading CT spotted us. Instantly he took aim at me and fired, but his shot whistled harmlessly past my body. Not giving him a second chance, I let off several rounds with my carbine. I saw him stagger and fall, so I knew my bullets had found their mark. Brown, too, was giving them the works. Also the other chaps were doing their best, especially Corporal Togom with his bren-gun. As we charged amongst them, our men were shouting 'Bunoh! - Bunoh!' ('Kill! Kill!').

Coming upon a mortally wounded CT I bent down to relieve him of his weapon. At that moment a sten-gunner, before I had the chance to stop him, fired a long burst at point-blank range into the man's head. His skull made a horrifying sound as bullets blasted it open. Just like a small explosion, his head burst apart, particles of brain spattered into my face, but I didn't care. A female CT started running towards one of her fallen comrades; I fired a couple of warning shots in her direction, but she carried on. In a flash she grabbed the dead man's weapon. As she was making her getaway, I took careful aim at her: I wanted to wound and capture, not kill. Gently I squeezed the trigger. She clutched her arm and let out a blood-curdling scream; I knew my aim had been a good one. As I tried for another shot I heard the familiar metallic click of an empty magazine. Before I had time to reload she had fled into the nearby jungle.

After the last shot had been fired, silence fell. We dragged the four dead bodies to the roadside and awaited police transport. Brown, myself and the chaps congratulated each other on our success. It seemed like a miracle that not one of us had been harmed.

Within fifteen minutes the police transport arrived. Callously, we flung the bullet-riddled CTs into the armoured car. Suddenly, the sight of their blood-soaked bodies filled me with disgust. I turned away and retched.

On our arrival at Cha'ah police station, the four dead men were soon identified as being the District Committee Member and some of his outfit. The woman who had escaped was Goh Peng Tuan's wife. Although she was a Communist and a terrorist, I could not help but admire her courage. Later, she was killed, along with him and many of his followers, when their camp was bombed by the RAF.

All the village seemed to turn out to stare at the corpses. Amongst the crowd I noticed the late District Committee Member's brother, so I made my way to where he was standing.

'Apparently your brother paid no heed to my message,' I said.

He didn't answer.

I then told him that if he was thinking of joining the Communists to seek revenge he had better think again. 'If you do,' I went on, 'these local people will be viewing *your* dead body, so remember my warning.' With that I left him to think it over.

Here I should say something about my platoon, for in jungle warfare, perhaps even more than in a 'conventional' battle, every man's life depends on the discipline, steadiness and trigger-sharp reactions of everyone else.

We usually patrolled in small units, ten or a dozen, lived on the same rice and dried fish, and mucked in together - and sometimes almost starved together - so the sense of comradeship was very strong, and differences of rank applied only in normal operational conditions.

My right-hand man while I was at Cha'ah was Sergeant Shaffie. He was a little chap, no more than 5'6", a Malay from Batu Pahat in Johore, and as soon as I met him I took to him. He was five years older than I, and like all Malays he smiled easily and often; but there was a steadiness and honesty about his face, especially in the eyes, which suggested great strength of character. When I arrived at Cha'ah he had already been a 'jungle cop' for five years. He had a fine record, and had no wish to return to normal police duties. No one was better at steadying the men when morale began to slip in appalling conditions, or when food was running out. Shaffie and I would often share our meagre rations, eating off the same leaf - washing up was not a problem in the jungle! - and drinking from the same water-bottle; but never did he take advantage of his position. What little English he spoke had a flavour all its own, and we normally conversed in Malay.

When we were on patrol he had a characteristic way of pointing out something. He didn't use his hand or his finger; instead, he would tilt his head back slightly, purse his lips and point his chin in the direction he wanted me to look, murmuring *'Sanah Tuan'* ('There, Sir'). I never had the least difficulty in seeing what he was indicating. When I called halt, I, and the others, would flop down exhausted, but not Shaffie. He would be off prowling around, searching for clues. He taught me a great deal about jungle-craft.

'Tuan, don't just look at the jungle round you. Try to look through it. Right through the tangle. You will see much further. Sniff the air for the smells of human habitation. Listen for the noises that don't belong'.

And it was true. By not simply staring at the immediate green curtains that closed us in all round, but by doing as he said, looking through it, you did see several yards further. Similarly, with use and training, all your senses become sharpened; you became, I suppose, that much closer to the instinctive reactions of aboriginal peoples. I was to see more of this later, when I was with the tribes in central Malaya; but it was Sergeant Shaffie who was my true mentor.

Another regular member of my 'team' was Jo-Jo, our cook, handyman, and, when occasion demanded, doctor. Jo-Jo was a Malay chinese, with that people's ability to adapt to any condition without complaint. Although he had had little contact with Europeans, he quickly fell in with my ways. At those times when I took only a small patrol out with me, Jo-Jo used to stay behind, which he hated as much as I did. I missed the mugs of hot tea he seemed to be able to produce under the most unlikely conditions. He also used to keep our encampments shipshape, and was in charge of the water point and the latrine. Jo-Jo was a country boy and improvisation was his forte; particularly with regard to cooking. The raw materials he had to work with were uninspiring - rice was the staple, with whatever else we could forage or carry - yet he did wonders with them. He was also our medicine man. In his pack he invariably carried that great cure-all 'Tiger Balm', as well as a variety of herbs, out of which he could quickly concoct evil, yet remarkably effective cures for our jungle maladies.

To look at, Jo-Jo was no beauty. His face, the colour of ancient teak, was long and pockmarked, and when he laughed he displayed several rather tarnished gold teeth. He had a large mole on his chin, out of which sprouted two long black hairs. As his jaw moved, these would flex and twitch, and I always saw them as the antennae of some insect that was busy fighting its way out. He was intensely proud of these two random whiskers. His eyes were small and black and sunk deep in their sockets, which gave him a look of great sagacity: an air of wisdom somewhat spoilt by his one serious weakness - gambling. In the camp I always knew where to find him - in the *basha* of the wireless operators, who were also Chinese, playing cards or mah-jong and, more often than not, losing his money. I did my best to discourage him; though if I saw that he was on a winning streak, I hadn't the heart - much to the disgust of the others. Jo-Jo would look at me sheepishly, and offer me a thimbleful of tea.

Out on patrol he was first-class; with his spindly legs and skeletal body and that dark, disfigured face of his, he was like some goblin or ancient spirit of the trees, and at the same time, since he was by far the oldest of us, something of a father figure. I could almost see him, after he'd left the force, setting up as some village wise man - except that I knew he'd be in the nearest tea-house clacking away with the mah-jong tiles.

Shaffie and Jo-Jo were the backbone of my platoon. The rest, mostly Malays, many of them hardly more than lads, all had their clearly defined characteristics and several of them will make their separate appearances later. They were a good bunch in a pretty grim trade, and they never let me down.

Weeks of intensive patrolling went by before I contacted CTs again. From my diary, written soon after the operation:

november 1953

On the last day of a week's hazardous operation, Sgt Shaffie located a CT track. By the condition of it, we estimated that it had last been used about 48 hours before. *Not knowing which direction led to their camp, we decided to lay an ambush. Taking care not even to snap the dew-laden spiders' webs that were hanging down and threaded about, Shaffie and I arranged our few men in position so that whichever way the CTs came we would achieve maximum kills. The spot was an ideal place for an ambush: the thick ferns and tangled undergrowth concealed our bodies perfectly. I briefed the men, saw that they were settled down, then positioned myself off the edge of the track behind a screen of foliage. I could see along it for about fifteen yards. Shaffie sat facing me, two yards away; he could observe the track in the opposite direction.*

Not a sound could be heard as we waited, except the chatter of monkeys in the distance. I wondered how may hours or even days we would have to sit there. Even then, perhaps, the CTs would not turn up.

As I sat picking the typhoid carrying rat ticks off my sweaty, filthy body, which hadn't been washed for a week, I heard the sound of deliberate, calculated movements some way down the narrow track. Swash, swash, swash. They were approaching slowly and with the utmost caution. Then a shadowy, khaki-clad figure slowly loomed out of the undergrowth. He was big and bulky for a Chinese. I nodded to Shaffie. The visual impact of seeing this armed terrorist bearing down the track to my position stunned me. Like a child's balloon in a gentle breeze, he drifted and weaved about, searching left and right, then up and down. His eyes were hawking about him all the time. From my cover I could with ease have taken him out, but I had to wait. He continued 'ballooning' as he cautiously shortened the distance between us, his rifle held at an oblique angle. With the track being only a footprint wide, I reckoned his rifle barrel would almost brush me as he passed and entered our trap. A second armed terrorist cradling a tommy-gun followed close behind him. The first one was only a matter of feet away from me now.

I froze as his rifle ruffled the undergrowth. My eyes were fixed on the barrel as it came closer and closer. I must not snap and blow the ambush. I wished I'd opened fire when he was several yards away, but then the other terrorist would have made good his escape. Now he was right opposite me; I could easily have reached out and touched him. I closed my eyes momentarily; when I opened them he was past. Now the second one was stealing towards me - was there a third? Through the heavy foliage I could see the single Communist star on his head gear, growing larger as he closed in. Still he did not know that unseen eyes were watching him.. It was a testing time for us all; if someone cracked now, I would be a goner.

I could hear him panting heavily. He gave a slight cough as he came right opposite me. It was time for action. I bounced to my feet and came face to face with him. His almond eyes filled with fear, and for a split second he appeared to be hypnotised with terror as we glared at each other. His mouth yawned wide open.

Suddenly the silence of the jungle was broken by his curdling, wailing cries, the screams of a man who knew he was doomed. He was at my mercy; he grappled for his tommy-gun to scythe me down, but I was too quick for him. Gritting my teeth, I fired a salvo from the hip. It was impossible to miss. As the bullets ripped into his body I shouted, 'Now cry, you bastard'. Instead of crumpling like

26

a puppet into a heap on the ground, he just stood there rocking back and forth. Was he going to fall on me, was he some kind of superman? Had my bullets struck his tommy-gun and ricocheted?. Or, with the carbine being of high muzzle velocity, had the bullets gone straight through him? How I wished I hadn't taken that dum dum round out of my carbine; that would have felled him. All this raced around my brain. I fired a second salvo into him. Clawing at me, he fell forward and, as he did so, I dodged back. He slumped on to the ground at my feet, mortally wounded. With one more shot I put him out of his misery.

The other CT had been killed outright by the bren-gunner. Both had been taken completely by surprise and hadn't even had a chance to fire their weapons. It was all over in seconds. The trees stood around like silent witnesses; the noise had shocked the monkeys into silence.

Shaffie reckoned that they had been out on an assassination mission - probably some wretched coolie had failed to pay his subscription to the party funds on time. The revolver on the tommy-gunner's belt would have been used for that job: instead, the exterminators had been exterminated. Shaffie and I discussed how it was they had failed to see me when I was only inches away. Shaffie grinned.

'Tuan, I was dying to break wind when they were close by you. If I had, they would have heard me, but they would have seen you.'

'True, Ghani, they would have spotted me for sure, were you shitting yourself?'

27

'Nearly Tuan, but I sure would have done if I'd been in your position!'

'It goes to prove that stillness is the art of camouflage. And it was a good job that no one broke the spiders' webs, this pair would have noticed for certain.'

'You're right, Tuan,' nodded Ghani.

Flies were already buzzing around the wounds. When I examined their weapons, I noticed that they had dumdum ammunition - common CT practice - and one of them had a handy-looking 'parang' inside his belt, far superior to our general issue. I took his for my own use, never thinking that it would help to save my life a few months later. The well-oiled revolver had most likely been taken from a British planter whom they had murdered. By the state of their footwear, puttees and uniforms, I estimated that they had left their camp only half an hour before. Men live and men die rapidly in this jungle warfare, I thought.

After we had taken a short rest, the men cut two straight branches, securely tied the hands and feet of the two dead men with rattan, then threaded the branches through the joined wrists and ankles. Thus, trussed up like animals, our prey was carried back to base camp. The men who had stayed behind were pleased to see us all return. They'd heard the firing, but could only guess who was ambushing whom. My first job was to send a radio message to the 10th Jungle Company HQ telling them of our success, and requesting transport to RV at a point north of Yong Peng.

After a mug of tea and a bite of food, we broke camp and headed for the main road. I was thankful that we were not too deep *in the jungle, otherwise carrying the bodies out would have proved difficult.*

By five pm we were at Company HQ. Assistant Superintendent of Police Fred Milner MC, the Commander, was there to greet us and very happy he was at the success of the operation. That evening Police Special Branch identified the two dead CTs as Kwee Loon, OC of a courier camp, and his bodyguard; they were carrying important documents.

Milner was just handing over his command at this time. We were all sorry when the time came for him to leave, as he was an excellent man to work under. On one occasion, when I was with Milner on an operation, I remember how he strolled into an occupied CT camp entirely unconcerned. The four CTs happened to be sitting with their backs to us. Instead of opening fire, Milner called on them to surrender. Far from doing so, they grabbed their weapons and a skirmish followed, and they made good their getaway. I can only think that he was too much of a gentleman to shoot anyone - even a CT - in the back.

Milner's hobby was gibbons. He kept two, and they were the most mischievous creatures I've ever come across, but very tame. One had the name of 'Mo Mo', the other 'Me Me'. They were rather fond of strong liquor and used to plunge their small hairy hands into someone's glass and scoop the contents into their mouths. They quite often got drunk, and the capers they cut then were hilarious.

After a good scrub and a square meal, Milner, Brown and I

walked over to the Oil Palm Estate Planters' Club, which was only about fifty yards away. The planters were a mixed bunch: British, French, Danish and Dutch. The drinking parties more often than not lasted all night, and if the following morning happened to be a Sunday, the ardent 'swillers' would make their way home for a quick shower and food, and return to the club for a few beers before their curry lunch.

This particular night I felt in a mood for getting 'blotto'. I was not in the same class, when it came to knocking them back, as the others there, so it didn't take many to achieve the desired effect. In the group at the bar was the wife of a planter. She was a typical 'Mem'[2], or thought she was. She turned to me, and addressed me in a rather haughty tone of voice.

'Mr Follows, however could you bear to kill those two men. Goodness, it seems so cruel!'

I kept my temper, and replied as calmly as I could, 'Someone has to help rid the country of the Communists.'

I thought of enlightening her a little by telling her that had it not been for our killing them and those like them, she would not have been enjoying herself at that moment; they would probably have been on their way to her bungalow to murder her and the rest of her family. I did not tell her this; I didn't want to spoil her sleep.

After everyone had had their fair quota of drink, someone suggested a dice game called 'The Drunken Coachman'. Foolishly, I agreed to join in. The first person to throw six aces orders any mixture of drink he likes. The second person to throw six aces has to pay for it, and the third unlucky blighter has to drink it. I was the 'unlucky blighter' in the first round. Some of the mixtures that were drunk during this game were incredible, and I'm sure that if there had been a tin of Brasso behind the counter that would have been included too. I managed to swallow the 'Devil's cocktail' dreamed up by the first chap and felt the room spinning round me. Very soon afterwards, I decided I had better leave. I staggered back to my quarters and threw myself onto the bed, there to sleep the sleep of the plastered for the rest of the night. It was one way of dissolving the tensions of an operation.

three

you are trapped and outnumbered - surrender!

Next morning I had a beauty of a hangover. 'Never again!' I thought. At least out on operations there would be no danger of getting into such a state. That morning, Brown departed for Johore Bahru hospital; his facial muscles had become increasingly paralysed and he should have gone sick weeks before, but he was keen to knock off a few more CTs first.

After a long spell in hospital he came back to the Jungle Company, but he seemed far from his usual self. Soon afterwards, he applied for the position of a planter on the nearby oil palm estate and was accepted; but when he requested to be released from the Malayan Police Force, they refused unless he bought himself out. Stupidly, he paid. Had he known the ropes, he could have been released for nothing and might even have secured a pension on the grounds of disability. The force certainly had its money's worth from P/Lt Brown. However, all worked out well in the end. He got married and settled down as a planter. It must bring back many memories to him as he goes round the estate where, at one time, he used to fight for his life, but where now, with the end of the guerrilla war in Malaya, all is peaceful - a point the 'memsahib' in the club might not fully appreciate.

My next three weeks were spent in retraining the platoon. The work included map-reading, range work, mock assaults on CT camps, Immediate Action drills (in case of our being ambushed) and other skills that might prove useful in jungle warfare.

Goh Peng Tuan had not been kicking his heels while we had been retraining. One night he led the 7th Independent Platoon in an attack on the Yong Peng Home Guard HQ and managed to get away with twenty or more weapons. A platoon of the Fijian Regiment, on the follow-up after the attack, soon located his platoon base. During the assault on the camp, the Fijians had two of their men killed and Goh Peng Tuan and his platoon escaped. CTs feared the courageous Fijians more than any other troops in Malaya. The Fijians' jungle ability was second to none and all of them were like oxen in physique. Their stamina in the hazardous jungle seemed to be inexhaustible. The 7th Independent Platoon must have been feeling rather proud of themselves, I thought, with these successes.

Several days after the Fijian skirmish, Major Golder, the Military Intelligence Officer, arrived at our HQ. He had driven the 40 miles from Segamat, so I knew his visit was important. He was soon telling us news of 0026. My heart seemed to miss a beat, as I knew that the code number was Goh Peng Tuan's. He went on to tell us that 0026 with his platoon, DCMs and their units from about six local villages, would be having their annual conference in about ten days' time, somewhere in the Maokil Forest Reserve. It was expected that there would be approximately sixty well-armed CTs at this meeting. My platoon happened to be the only one available at the time, so I was to go out in search of their camp. What would take place if we happened to come across it could be anyone's guess.

november 1953

The platoon and I were cautiously slogging our way through the Maokil area. I had an SEP (Surrendered Enemy Personel) with me and I made him do the difficult and dangerous task of leading scout; if we happened to be ambushed, the first chap would nearly always be the first to be killed, and naturally I would sooner see an ex CT dead than any of my own men. At one place he pointed out to me where he, along with a strong force of CTs, had ambushed and killed a number of British soldiers some time before. As I walked behind him I noticed his animal-quick instincts and reactions, acquired through years spent being hunted in the jungle. During the Japanese occupation of Malaya, he served with the Malayan Peoples' Anti-Japanese Army. In 1948, at the beginning of the Malayan emergency, he joined the communist Malayan Races Liberation Army (the MRLA) and remained in the organisation for some years until he finally surrendered himself to one of our sections.

We spent a total of four days trekking, every minute on the alert. On the fifth day we made our base camp and DZ (Dropping Zone). It was situated at the confluence of two small rivers, which gave us a certain amount of natural defence. On the first day we found the tracks of three CTs. We estimated the tracks to be quite fresh, only a few hours old. All our skill was used in trying to follow them, but we failed.

Airdrop day arrived. Two parachutes became entangled in the branches of huge trees, one of which we had to fell. Having in our possession only parangs for the job, it took almost three hours. A couple of agile men climbed the other tree and cut free the crate containing the supplies from the parachute. At all times we are at the ready in base camp and whilst out patrolling. All conversation is carried on in whispers. I allow wood-cutting and collecting twigs for lighting fires to be done only one hour of the day, in the early morning. Sounds of wood-cutting travel far in the jungle and many a camp position has been given away by SF (Security Forces) and CTs alike through this noise. I curse softly at any man who clangs his mess-tin or water-bottle. 'Stand to' is carried out religiously each dawn and dusk. We do not intend to be caught with our pants down.

A week of intense patrolling went by and still we found no further signs of Communists. I began to wonder whether the information we had been given was 'duff'. The day of our airdrop came round once more, but nothing arrived. Wanting to know the reason, I spoke to someone in HQ by radio. I was informed that we had already received our supplies. I almost exploded with rage.

'Would I be making inquiries if we had already received them?' I asked.

Finally, I was told to expect them the following day.

Once again we waited in vain. By then we were almost on a starvation diet. A few men had the odd tin of meat, some had very little rice and an ounce or two of tea. Collecting the bits together, I rationed them out the best I could to the whole platoon. Even the river nearby did not offer us any fish because of its shallowness; the traps and snares which we laid around our camp in the hope of catching some wild animal yielded nothing. A few of the chaps went out in search of anything edible, but all they brought back was a type of fungus similar to our mushroom which grows on the dead trunks of fallen trees. At first I was very reluctant to eat them, but being so ravenously hungry I decided to chance it.

Once again I reminded HQ by radio of our plight. Their answer was the same as before. Expect airdrop tomorrow.' The morrow arrived. It looked like being the third day without a decent meal. I noticed one or two of the men, and even myself, were beginning to get edgy through lack of food. How I wished Milner were still in command. Without hesitation he would have organised an 'Auster' aircraft to 'free drop' enough food just to keep the wolf from the door.

A quarter of a mile away from our HQ was an airstrip for light planes designed to be used for such emergencies. On this occasion it was not made use of. By the afternoon we had just about lost faith in our HQ staff, so I sent a curt message saying that we would be starting our return journey at first light in the morning. That night I found it most difficult to sleep. My head was splitting through lack of food and I felt weak. I'm sure that I would have devoured a mangy dog if there had been one anywhere around. After lying there for what seemed like hours, tortured by thoughts of food, I must have dozed off.

Before first light the following morning the men had packed their kits. There was no cooking to be done, so in a very short time we were on the move - due east; this meant we would be in for some rough terrain. I expected to arrive at the main road before darkness fell in twelve hours' time.

For the first hour there was no incident; the men all did

exceptionally well in keeping up their spirits. From experience, I knew this could not continue, and that very soon a number of them would start fainting through sheer weakness. Pulling ourselves up the steep and slippery hills was draining us of the little energy we had left. After a while the men began to collapse, not surprisingly as it was now over three days since any of us had eaten. Sergeant Shaffie who, as always, was full of stalwartness, stayed behind with any unfortunate man who went down. He helped him on his way after the man had recovered. Very soon I was burdened with someone else's pack besides my own; the man I took it from was just about on his last legs. As we struggled on, I did all I could to coax the rest of the platoon not to give in.

Before long even I began to feel the strain. Coloured spots and lines began to cloud my vision, my head throbbed and I found it difficult to concentrate on the navigation or to think sensibly. I found myself unable to keep my feet and often fell heavily, cursing as I did so.

It was now eleven o'clock. My previous calculations indicated that by eleven am we should have been clear of the jungle-clad hills that were still facing us. However, we continued on our same course. At midday an apprehensive feeling of being lost in this colossal rain forest began to nag at me. I was sure that I'd been using the compass correctly, or had I? Sergeant Shaffie and I discussed the predicament; his thoughts were much the same as mine - we were lost. For a minute or two my thoughts ran wild, thinking of the horrible consequences which might happen to us.

We had to get out of that green hell or another day without

food would see some of the men unable to carry on. The platoon, I knew, always trusted me to get us out of any such difficulties; we'd shared a number together, but his time I could not guarantee the outcome and I felt wholly responsible for our plight. I was quite confident we were still moving east, which was our course. As we pressed on I consulted my compass more regularly; we deviated maybe a few degrees north or south, but our general direction remained constant.

By three o'clock we were still among the slippery, jungle-covered hills and travelling at a snail's pace. Halting the platoon for a rest, Shaffie and I pondered over our maps, trying to fix our position. As we were so engaged, a member of the platoon came up to us and spoke rapidly to Shaffie. They conversed far too quickly for me to understand fully but, seeing a look of astonishment spread over Shaffie's face, I gathered something was wrong. Climbing to his feet, Shaffie made his way amongst the platoon until he was out of my view. Hearing his raised voice, I went to see if there was any trouble. Shaffie was dressing down one of the men. He turned to me.

'This man is responsible for our being lost, Sir, not you.'
'Why is that?'

He showed me a piece of rotan and a small rock that he had taken off the man. These two articles, he said, are not the ordinary sort, but of a kind which supposedly holds magical powers. Malay people, he continued, never attempt to take them away from the jungle, as they belong to the jungle devil; he will prevent anyone who tries to steal them from leaving his domain.

The man told us that he wanted the things to give to his kampong bhomo - village witchdoctor - on his return there. He knew he was taking a chance in trying to bring them out of the jungle. With that, he threw them as far as possible down the hill we'd just climbed. Shaffie and the men were convinced that very soon we should once again be able to fix our position.

Sure enough, within ten minutes, we found ourselves on a disused woodcutter's track with which we were all familiar. This wasn't the first time I'd come up against the Malays' superstitions, but I still don't understand it. Was it coincidence, or had the 'jungle devil' really freed us? I often wonder. What a relief it was to have shaken off the fear of being lost and to know that within about two hours we should be on the main road. There we would have transport to our HQ, where we could get some food.

The SEP, who was the leading scout, suddenly halted without warning. Instinct told me that he had seen something important. yes, down the track where he was pointing were several nibong trees which had only recently been cut down, probably that same morning; there were also a large number of fresh footprints which must have been left by CTs. I knew they were from the camp we'd been searching for. Neither the men nor myself were in a fit state to launch an assault. Shaffie and I had a short parley on the best thing to do. We both knew it would be useless to take men who were continually fainting, so the only solution was to sort out the fittest men.

In all, we mustered nine chaps: Shaffie himself, the SEP, six members of the platoon and me. Nine starving men against fifty tough CTs - what hope had we? But there was no other choice. Shaffie noticed my uneasiness.

'Well, Tuan, what do you think? Shall we attack or not?'

I glanced at him and said calmly, 'We'll attack the camp.'

Before our small outfit moved off, I gave orders for the rest of the platoon not to leave their position under any circumstances until we returned. When that would be, or even how many of us would be returning, I couldn't say; but I had to be certain that any movement we might hear, and any figures we might see, would be from the CTs and not our own men. Shaffie and I took leading scout alternately. We moved slowly and with extreme caution. The track was very easy to follow, as it had been used so many times by many CTs, and I knew we were heading for the lion's den.

For a quarter of a mile or more we followed the twists and turns of the track. Our main object was to try to spot their sentry before he spotted us. Every five or six yards we stopped to listen and search for any tell-tale signs of a sentry post.

Now it was my turn to lead. I knelt behind some foliage and peered down the track. Systematically I searched first the left side then the right. My nerves were almost at breaking point. All I could see was a tangled mass of greenery. Slowly I climbed to my feet and gingerly moved forward. I had only gone about four paces when, without warning, a shot rang out right ahead. It was their sentry. For a split second my mind went blank: then, springing to my feet, I yelled 'Charge!' and dashed down the track.

Before we'd gone fifteen yards we came under heavy fire from an assortment of weapons. I threw myself down and shouted *to the men to do the same. The enemy's bullets were ripping through the air, far too close for my liking. We exchanged a fusillade. As their firing intensified from the front, it also came from our left and right flanks. They were trying to encircle us ready for the kill. Quickly I regrouped the men, positioning one bren-gun to cover our rear and to open fire at any movement in that direction. It was lucky I had ordered the remainder of the platoon not to move; they would have heard all the firing, but would be helpless to do anything about it. At this point I exchanged my carbine for the other brengun. Sergeant Shaffie kept signalling to the men not to bunch together; a hand-grenade thrown by the CTs would inflict several casualties and we could not afford to lose a single man.*

The SEP was the nearest man to me; I could only catch glimpses of the others. They looked grim. Corporal Yacob gave me a weak smile which I returned with a 'thumbs up' sign. Hussain quietly intoned a prayer to Allah. Sergeant Shaffie was his usual cool calm self, and this steadied the whole section.

I thought of the 'thin red line' - ours might have been the thin green one! With the bren, I returned the CTs' fire with several short bursts. As I stood there, firing from the hip (the tripods are of no use in close-quarter combat), with the butt recoiling in my hip, I felt somewhat less vulnerable. Then as though a film director had ordered 'cut', the firing stopped; yet I had given no order. A strong smell of cordite hung in the dark jungle air. As we crouched, expecting them to charge, I checked my hand-grenade and parang. I strained my ears for any tell-tale noise, but all was fearsomely quiet.

Then, to my utter astonishment, the unnatural silence was broken, not by the blare from their bugler, followed by a screaming charge, but by a voice calling on us to surrender, as we were trapped and outnumbered. The weird voice echoed through the jungle, taunting us. It seemed so close; but I could see no movement. The SEP gazed at me in terror and jibbered that it was none other than Goh Peng Tuan, commander of the ruthless 7th Independent Platoon, the elite, the crack unit of the Communists in Johore. The 7th must have been full of confidence, after a run of successful engagements against the Security Forces. Only three weeks before they had fought a pitched battle with a full platoon of Security Forces and inflicted very heavy casualties on them. I waited a few seconds before shouting back that we would fight it out, and I underlined my answer with a couple of burst of bren fire.

Their response was much as I expected; they threw everything at us, automatic fire and grenades. The jungle was at that point our only ally. How often I'd cursed it, but I was all praise for it in that situation: the trees, saplings and tangled undergrowth absorbed all their fire; the swampy ground took the impact of the grenades which they hurled at us. Their concentrated firing was scything down branches which fell amongst us.

Another lull followed, then the same haunting voice called out to us again. The closeness disturbed me. Next the voice suggested that the men should turn me over to them in return for their own lives. I knew what my fate would be if Goh Peng Tuan got his hands on me; no doubt he knew that I had wounded his wife in a previous encounter. His speciality is hacking off limbs, especially fingers for rings. He is a psychopath and an evil, ruthless killer.

Ever since I learnt what CTs do to their prisoners, I never wear jewellery. A watch is a must, but no rings, neck chains, or bracelets; I do not even have a dog tag around my neck; not even a wallet with personal papers or letters from loved ones - nothing on me at all except the barest necessities[3].

I glanced at the men. I'd shared meagre rations with them on many occasions, shared good and bad times alike. We'd known each other for quite some time. When some of the men yelled back and continued firing, I knew they wouldn't desert me. The SEP knew what would happen to him if he was captured, and so he kept blasting away with his 303. I roared back at the voice, 'Stay and fight, you bastards!', at the same time shouting out commands to imaginary sections, making out there was a full platoon of us or more, instead of only nine men. The CTs would have heard my commands, but would they fall for the deception? At the same time we laid down heavy fire and, shouting at the top of our voices, charged several yards forward in the direction of the voice. Their return fire appeared to be less aggressive.

As we edged slowly forward I saw the rood of a basha only about twenty-five yards away. About midway between us and the basha was a huge fallen tree, which would afford us ample cover. Their firing had become sporadic. A quick twisting run, and I hurled myself at the fallen tree. My body jolted to a halt; I was safely tucked in behind it.

In no time Shaffie was there with me. A quick check of our ammunition; I had one full magazine - twenty-eight rounds - in my pouch, plus a few rounds in the magazine. Shaffie had twenty-five rounds left for his carbine. Resting the bren on the top of the tree trunk, I took aim at the basha and let loose several single shots until the magazine was empty. Snapping the last one in position and placing the lever back to automatic, I felt safe in the sanctuary behind this cover; I did not want to move.

Most of the men were by now up to, or near, the fallen tree. Miraculously we hadn't suffered a single casualty. 'Keep praying Hussain,' I said to myself. Then I vaulted over the tree trunk and, firing the bren all the while, I rushed up the slight incline into their camp. There, standing in the centre of it, I went berserk, letting loose all round me with the bren. I was elate, drunk with victory.

One of the men shouted 'Tuan kiri sana!' ('Sir, left there!). I swung to my left; there was a movement in the jungle. I squeezed the trigger only to hear the metallic click of the empty magazine! Shaffie quickly snapped off a couple of shots in that direction. There we were, in a Communist stronghold and out of ammunition. We couldn't stay in the camp, it might have been a trap; if they counter-attacked, we would have little chance.

We went straight through the camp and waited for several minutes just on the edge, listening and watching. The fire was still smouldering, cooking the unattended meal. Now my hunger came back to me; the smell of food was tantalising. After a time we warily went back into the camp. There were several large pools of blood, so we know that we must have wounded some of them. Good.

The camp had accommodated about fifty men. We searched

round and found a sack of sugar. It was all too much for me; I started to stuff handfuls of it into my mouth. Soon my straggly beard became a gooey, sticky mess. We set fire to the camp, and set off back along the track. Soon we were reunited with the remainder of the platoon. We had brought the sack of sugar with us, and it soon disappeared.

They had, of course, heard the firing, and most of them had never expected us to return. Some had wanted to come to our aid, but knowing the difficulty of distinguishing friend from foe in the jungle they had obeyed my orders and stayed put, which was just as well. Now, it's head for the main road, get on the radio and ask for transport to take us back to headquarters, to a bath and a decent meal.

That skirmish had a sequel which, though amusing to look back on, made my blood boil at the time. There was a new CO at Rengam, fifty miles away and conveniently close to Singapore. When he received the news he sent for me. I went down by Land Rover, entered his office and saluted. He was reading a letter and did not bother to acknowledge the salute.

'H'm,' I thought, 'I've come across your type before.'

After some time he put down the letter and glared at me with a steady eye.

'Ah, Follows. What's all this about your attacking a CT camp and killing none of them, eh?'

His voice sounded as if his mouth were full of ball bearings, and I started bristling immediately.

'If we'd been properly supplied, as requested.' I said, ' and if I'd had more than eight extremely hungry men, I dare say we should have done better. As it was, we were lucky to get away as lightly as we did - and inflict casualties on them into the bargain.'

'I'd have thought you could have got some of them, just the same,' he said, and mumbled on about how damned awkward it was going to be for him to explain it to his pals in the club.

It would have been far less embarrassing for him, or course, if we'd all been wiped out, but this intrepid office warrior had never been near the jungle. If I hadn't excused myself and left his office then, I might have done something I would have regretted afterwards. Mercifully, although I served in the same unit for many more months, I never came across him again; but I did sometimes wonder how the poor fool managed to explain our 'lapse' away to his chums. From time to time we would suffer from types like him, and a pain in the arse they were.

For a few nights after this encounter, I had difficulty in sleeping. My mind was in turmoil and I had vivid nightmares. The answer, I thought, might be to return to the scene of the action, and this I did after a few days. I went through the whole thing again, in my mind and on the ground, reliving every tense moment. Afterwards I felt more relaxed; and when people asked me why, under the circumstances, I hadn't retreated instead of standing firm and then attacking, I could honestly say that it had never occurred to me. But it did leave me badly shaken for nearly a week, and I'm sure that if I hadn't exorcised it by going back, the jungle would have beaten me.

four

hand to hand

Early in 1954 there was a reorganisation which affected the 10th Police Jungle Company: we were amalgamated with three other companies to form the 4th Police Field Force. HQ was at Kulai, seventy five miles north of Johore Bahru, and roughly midway between there and Yong Peng. But it did not make any difference to operations: there were companies at Rengam, Cha'ah and elsewhere, and our normal patrol unit was still the platoon.

In June I had a feeling that it would be worth investigating the Sungei Kemadak area. No Security Forces had been there for some months; and its mountains, heavy jungle and deep valleys were ideal CT territory. Through it flowed the Sungei Kemadak, which was fed by innumerable swift torrents from the surrounding hills.

To get there meant a gruelling trek, and it took us two and a half days to reach our operational area. At the end of that time we came to the banks of the river, and I established our base camp there. On the very first patrol we came upon evidence of CTs in the vicinity, but it took four days of patient, painstaking tracking before we located their camp.

Led by our two aborigine trackers, we followed the river as it twisted through the jungle. The water level was low, with sandy beaches here and there. A couple of times I drew the attention of the trackers to places where the sand had been disturbed, but they confidently assured me that it was caused by birds scratching about. At first I took their word for it; but after a time, as we came upon more of these 'bird scratchings', I decided to clamber down to the river for a closer look. At the water's edge I could just make out toe prints in the sand. It was enough, the tell-tale sign: we were on to them. Shaffie and the two trackers joined me by the river.

'What sort of large bird has claws like that?' I asked the trackers and they looked distinctly sheepish. I felt good, one up to me, the city type doing their work for them!

It's impossible to actually track in a river, but every so often we came across sandy islets, and on these we found fresh footprints obviously made by CTs. We were doing well, then we lost the trail. Somewhere they had left the river. We carried on, searching every inch of the river bank, without success. After a time we arrived at a waterfall and I called a halt for a rest. There were masses of fish in the clear water, and I decided to drop a hand-grenade so we could all enjoy fresh fish for tea. I was just preparing to throw it when Shaffie hurried over making signs for silence. He had picked up the trail again only yards from where we were resting. It was well used and easy to follow. They were so confident that no one would find their hide-out in the deep jungle that they had even built a foot-bridge across one of the streams. From the far side we could see their camp. It was on the edge of a large cultivated vegetable plot. Looking across towards their camp, I thought how hard they must have worked to clear the jungle to grow food for themselves.

To assault the camp from where we were would have been suicidal, as we could have been picked off quite easily once we were in the open. Besides, we had no means of knowing how many of them there were, though we estimated not more than ten. We kept the camp under observation for some time, and we heard wood being chopped. I was filled with excitement at the thought that we would soon be engaging the enemy in battle.

'OK, Shaffie,' I said. 'I will take half the men with me and try to make my way to the rear of their camp and attack it from there. When you hear us firing, you and your party open up into their camp with everything you've got.'

We synchronised watches; assault time was to be in three-quarters of an hour, which should have allowed us time to get into position. If by that time no firing came from my party, it meant that I was in a worse position than Shaffie, and he was to attack the camp with his group. Looking up to the sky I hoped for rain, as it would deaden our movements. Leaving Shaffie with seven men, I slowly and cautiously led my seven around the edge of the vegetable garden. After twenty minutes we still had quite a long way to go - were we going to make it in time?

14/15 june 1954

About twenty-five yards of neatly hoed and growing vegetables separated us from the nearest basha. I was lying on the ground observing the camp, when I saw a CT come out of a basha and gaze across to where we were. The thick green foliage hid us from his prying eyes. Should I open fire on him? He was an easy target from my position and I couldn't miss. It was too late; he moved out of my line of fire.

I took the bren-gun and, telling the chaps to cover me, left the cover of the jungle. Slowly, flat on my belly, I snaked across the open vegetable plot, a perfect target. The rain which I was hoping for hadn't arrived; instead, I could feel the sun beating down on my back. I moved ever so slowly, first pushing the bren in front of me, then moving alongside it.

I was in the centre of open ground when an armed CT appeared from behind a basha. He was only ten yards away. My finger curled around the bren's trigger. I felt horribly naked lying there without cover, even though I knew that as he stood there, gazing around, my men had him in their sights. If he was to see me and make a move for his weapon, they would open fire.

As I watched, he stretched and scratched himself, then he loudly cleared his throat and spat in my direction. Had he followed the trajectory of his spit, he would have seen me, but no, he just scratched again and strolled back. I decided I would rather not get caught lying down if any of his chums decided to come over for a good spit, so I climbed to my feet, hugging my bren butt well into my hip, and very cautiously walked towards the bashas. The first one I came to was deserted. I peered round the corner; there were two armed CTs with their backs to me. Stealthily, I closed the distance between us. I was very close to them, and still they didn't realise I was there. I did not intend to miss. I took stock of them for a few seconds. One of them was smoking and I decided to take him first.

I aimed the bren, which I could just about keep steady, then whistled. He turned around. Surprise and horror disfigured the man's face. He held his hands with palms towards me as if to ward off the bullets which he knew would be ripping into his body at any moment. Slowly he started to walk backwards; then he turned to run. At that second I squeezed the trigger; the bren bucked against my hip. He performed a grotesque dance as the bullets spun him round, and then his legs gave way and he crumpled to the ground with the blood trickling from his wounds. As I turned the bren on to the second CT, I was met by a hail of fire. It came from Shaffie and his men, who could not see me, but were carrying out my orders to shoot up the camp as soon as they heard firing.

As I dodged this unwelcome fusillade and went after the second CT, I stumbled and fell, dropping the bren. I was afraid to stop in case I got caught by my own men's fire. I ran like hell after the CT, who must have believed he could escape. I threw myself on his back. We went sprawling; my hands grappled for his throat. His fingers were gouging at my eyes. Screaming and fighting back, he managed to break my stranglehold.

As we rolled over and over, I knew we were about evenly matched. He was as lithe and tough as a jungle cat, but I too was fit and pretty nimble - I needed to be for I'm only nine stone and we were both fighting for our lives. In the navy I'd been in brawls in ports around the world, but his was different.

Then he tried to release the hand-grenade attached to his belt; he knew the hangman's rope awaited him if he was captured alive, and he was quite prepared to blow himself up as well as me.

At all costs I had to keep his hands away from it. By now, we were both screaming at each other, our faces often only three inches apart. His breath smelled vile, and he had a wicked-looking scar across his chin and small, darting, pig-like eyes. As we rolled over we punched, kneed, kicked, and clawed at each other. I could feel a knife fastened to the back of his belt. Suddenly I remembered my own parang, the one I'd taken from a dead CT a few weeks previously. I managed to draw it from its scabbard. Astride his body, I tried desperately to cut his throat. Each time I succeeded in getting the blade to his neck, he fought back like a cornered rat, forcing my hand away. This was not one of those bloodless Hollywood duels, this was real - his death or mine!

Now, in an attempt to get the knife away from me, he clutched the blade: quickly and deliberately I drew the knife through his hand. He yelled with pain. His fingers were lacerated but there was still plenty of fight left in him. Frantically I stabbed at him and each time he thrashed about and screamed with pain. It took all my strength to plunge the knife into his writhing body. At last he began to weaken and the fight drained out of him.

I raised the knife to finish him off, but at that moment our eyes met. He was in my power and he knew it: his eyes pleaded for mercy - I paused. We were both young; what would he have done if he had been in my place? How many men, women and children had he helped to kill? The thoughts ran through my mind: Chinese against British, Communism against democracy, him against me. Perhaps he'd been tricked into joining the Communist party and was not one at heart.

In that instant of doubt, I wish I hadn't looked into those eyes. I made as if to plunge the knife between his ribs and, as his hands went there to protect himself, I hit him hard between the eyes with the back of the blade and knocked him out. For a second before the blood began to flow I saw the gleaming whiteness of his skull. Slowly I raised myself from his body and stood up, watching the blood ooze out and channel its way across his forehead, to drip on to the leaf-covered ground. I relieved him of his grenade and knife. Shaffie warily appeared.

'Tuan - are you all right?'

'Yes I am'.

We called for the platoon medical orderly, who rushed breathlessly up, took one look at the blood-covered and still unconscious CT, and went deathly pale. Some medical orderly, fainting at his first sight of blood! I took the medical satchel from him and dressed the man's wounds myself. After a bit the CT came to and asked for water. I held my bottle to his lips. No funny business, I told him, or he'd end up like his friend - dead.

His name, I discovered, was Ng Aik Peng and they were the only two in the camp when we attacked. Five of his comrades had left on a foraging expedition only half an hour before I fired the first shot - our bad luck. He could not walk because of the knife wound I had inflicted in the small of his back, so an improvised stretcher had to be made to carry him back to our base camp.

Someone had blown the top off the other man's head with a bren, as neatly as if a circular saw had been used for the job. Before he was trussed to a pole in the usual way, his head, or what was left of it, had to be tied up in an old shirt to stop his brains dropping out.

I decided not to destroy the camp and the vegetable plot, for my idea was to ambush it when the others returned from their expedition, probably in three or four day's time. It was an ideal spot for ambushing, and 'kills' were certain.

It took us four hours to get back to our base camp by the river. The rest of the platoon were pleased at our success; they had not heard the firing.

We left the dead CT in the DZ; the other, Ng, we made as comfortable as possible close to my *basha*. The lads make quite a fuss of him, giving him cigarettes, chocolates and tea, and towards me he was friendly and answered any questions I asked him.

That evening I sent a message to HQ: 'COMMUNIST CAMP ATTACKED. ONE CT KILLED, ONE CAPTURED, CAPTURED SUFFERING FROM KNIFE WOUNDS. REQUEST HELICOPTER TO LIFT OUT DEAD AND CAPTURED CT.'

Early the following morning we started to turn the DZ into an LZ (Landing Zone). With all the felled trees, the camp soon looked more like a lumber site than a jungle base. Meanwhile we did not relax our vigilance.

At approximately eleven thirty the following morning a Royal Navy helicopter arrived to settle delicately down amongst the stumps of the trees; from it stepped Assistant Superintendent Roy Henry[4]. His reason for flying in was to see for himself that I had captured the CT first, and hadn't stabbed him later in order to obtain information from him. There were certain people who were quite ready to suspect the worst. It told him the story of how I had captured Ng and, as I was doing so, the men placed the dead CT in a large coffin-shaped wicker basket which was suspended beneath the helicopter. By this time the dead man's face was a seething mass of ants. The captured CT was helped aboard and within ten minutes the chopper was threshing its way back to Segamat.

That afternoon I received a wireless message: 'RETURN SOONEST TO TAC HQ. SOMETHING HOT.' As we were already on to a red-hot thing of our own, with the planned ambush of the camp, and as we were expecting our airdrop within twenty-four hours, I was not pleased. I was even less pleased when I got back to HQ. That night Sergeant Shaffie and I racked our brains as to what the message meant.

No sooner had we broken camp than we heard the familiar drone of the supply aircraft. The pilot spent ages searching for us, weaving along the valleys, dodging mountains in the most hair-raising manner. No one, it seemed, had bothered to inform the RAF that we had been withdrawn.

Our packs were so light that our return journey to HQ was made in double-quick time. On arrival at HQ I dismissed the platoon and went to find out what was so 'hot' that it demanded our instant return - to be told that it had been simply a device to get the platoon back quickly, and that after reporting in I would have to go back to the Kemedek area the next day. After such a cock-up, I had no intention of returning there just like that, and I said so, forcibly. The person who had ordered us back realised that he had made a real mess of things; but instead of being reprimanded, he was shortly afterwards promoted, and posted soon after that. Had we stayed put in the Kemedek area, I'm sure we should have achieved more kills.

When Ng Aik Peng's trial for his life came up, Sergeant Shaffie, a couple of the men and I had to attend court. As I gave my evidence from the box, I felt that it might have been better for everyone, especially him, if I had finished him off instead of taking him alive. As he proclaimed his innocence while being sentenced to death, I could not help but feel sorry for him.

After he was led away, Mr Justice Storr asked me to stand. I thought I was going to be ticked off for something or other. Instead he congratulated me for what he termed 'a brave act'. I suppose Ng Aik Peng would have been similarly congratulated by his side if the fight had gone the other way.

The affair was reported in the *Straits Times*, but only very briefly. I was warned not to speak to the Press, and was whisked away directly after the trial to make sure I didn't. I wasn't even allowed to visit Ng in hospital before the trial. The reason for it being played down was an earlier case involving a female CT by the name of Lee Ming. She had been captured in rather similar circumstances, and she had also carried a grenade - something which automatically carried the death penalty. She had been tried, found guilty, and condemned to death. Because she was a woman, this had caused an almighty stink all over the world, and her sentence was finally commuted to one of life imprisonment. As a result, the authorities had become wary of advertising the fact that the death penalty was being employed in the war against terrorism in Malay.

In an even more extraordinary case in which I was involved, two more members of the 5th Independent Platoon, who were captured later during an SOVF (Special Operational Volunteer Force) operation, were never even brought to trial and got away scot-free. Whether this was because they persuaded the authorities to give them SEP status, I don't know, but to me it smacked of a double standard. Why should Ng Aik Pen hang while the other three got away with their lives?

A week after the operation, I received the following 'Letter of Commendation' from the Commissioner of Police, W.L.R. Carbonell:

I have great pleasure in awarding you this Letter of Commendation for Merit in recognition of the extremely efficient and conscientious manner in which you have carried out your duties as a platoon commander in No.4 Police Field Force.

I have been particularly pleased to hear of the way in which you have frequently volunteered for extra patrol duties, even when you have just returned from a long patrol, and of the example which you have set by your disregard for your personal comfort.

21 June 1954.

W.L.R Carbonell. Commissioner of Police

Federation of Malaya, Kuala Lumpur

five

dead fish and frog-piss

The village of Cha'ah was one of more than five hundred built during the emergency. Called the 'new villages', they were the inspiration of General Templer's predecessor, Sir Henry Gurney. Their purpose was to sever communication between the terrorists and those Malays and Chinese who lived in scattered communities on the fringes of the jungle, and who could be compelled, by threats and intimidation, to supply the CTs . The plan involved moving these vulnerable people into newly created, self-sufficient villages surrounded by barbed wire, the purpose of which was to keep the CTs out as much as to keep the villagers in. The perimeter fence was regularly patrolled by sections of Malay Police and by and large, the scheme was successful.

Information reached me in July 1954 that certain CTs were getting through the wire at Cha'ah, going to the home of a Communist sympathiser, and receiving supplies of food from him. First, I set an ambush to try and catch the intruders, but when, after three nights of lying up in the bush, I had no result, I decided to try a different approach. Four of us would climb through the wire dressed in CT uniform. One, a Chinese by the name of PC Tan, would then enter the house and ask if they knew the whereabouts of his comrades, as he had lost contact with them that morning after being ambushed. He would be unarmed as he had lost his rifle in the ambush. I found out from the Station Sergeant and Cha'ah how long it took one of his armed sections to patrol the perimeter, but didn't tell him why I wanted to know. If I had taken the patrol off for a night, it would have aroused suspicion. We would have roughly an hour, after quietly sneaking through the barbed wire, before the police section completed their round. The idea was to be through the wire and out again while they were out of the way. During this time, Tan would be trying to find out the intruder's movements. If we got it wrong and the patrol spotted us, they would surely open fire. We wore training shoes in preference to jungle boots which, with their heavy barred rubber soles, leave an unmistakable footprint and would announce that Security Forces were in the area. If I left the slightest hint of evidence around the suspect's house, my cover would be blown.

So, armed with a sawn-off shotgun, a sten-gun and two carbines, the four of us made our way to a point near the high double barbed-wire fence. It was a bright moonlit night. There was no sound from the village except for the occasional barking dog, for there was a strict curfew. We kept out of sight and waited. Soon we heard the police squad making their round. They passed. As soon as they were out of earshot, we began our assault on the fence. This proved to be more troublesome and time-consuming than I'd bargained for. Once through, we ghosted our way amongst the dwelling to the suspect's house.

Another thing I hadn't taken into account was the possibility of a guard-dog. As we approached, I heard a deep, slow, throaty growl and the next thing I knew this huge beast was baring its fangs at me and leaping to the full length of its tether. This was a signal for all the dogs in the compound to create havoc. For several minutes the moonlit silence was rent by barking and howling dogs; even the pigs in the sty, where I was crouching, joined in the chorus.

Gradually the barking ceased and stillness returned. PC Tan passed me his carbine, then knocked sharply on the door several times. It slowly creaked open. The occupant, seeing a bedraggled CT standing there, quickly ushered him inside and smartly closed the door.

'First phase OK.' I whispered to Shaffie.

I had taken up a position round the corner from the door, with the sawn-of shotgun at the ready in case there were armed CTs already in the house. However, all I could hear as I listened at the door was a muffled conversation taking place between PC Tan and the occupier, and the sound of cooking utensils. PC Tan had no watch with him for he was supposed to be a lowly member of the Communist organisation who could not afford one. I had therefore suggested he should plead for a cigarette as soon as possible after entering the house, and when he had finished it he would leave, having thought up some excuse during his conversation with the sympathiser. Fifteen minutes passed. Any time now Tan should reappear. I listened by the door: more sounds, this time of eating.

Shaffie tugged at my sleeve; he could hear the police approaching on their rounds. They were so close we could pick up snatches of their conversation. Our only cover was by the pigsty. The three of us huddled there together as the sound of their footsteps grew louder and louder. They were right opposite us now.

What if Tan were to emerge at this moment? Then the dog started barking again, and footsteps came to a halt no more than a yard or two from where we were crouched. '*Babi*' ('pig') I overheard one of them mutter; as good Moslems, they would probably not investigate the sty. *'Anjang diam!'* ('Dog, quiet!') one shouted; and they moved on.

Several minutes later we heard movements from the house, and Tan emerged - at last. Silently he joined us; no words were exchanged. We flitted back, like phantoms, the way we had come, amongst the sleeping shanties. In one of them a light flickered and I peered in; through a haze of smoke I could see three or four Chinese in a state of oblivion. We left them in peace to smoke their *chandue* (opium).

The wire fence did not delay us as long this time, and moving fast we were soon back in our barracks. Over a cup of tea, Shaffie and I de-briefed PC Tan. He had been welcomed with great hospitality and given a meal.

'You were supposed to smoke one cigarette and leave,' I said, 'not settle down for the night!' I pretended to be angry.

'But , Sir, I was enjoying the meal!' Tan said, ' and I got some useful information.'

Apparently the CTs had visited the house on several occasions, the last time only three nights before. They were from the Sun Tian Kang area.

'Did you find out when they're over again?'

'I tried to, but he couldn't tell me. He didn't know, Sir.'

'OK Tan, you did a splendid job!'

'Yes Sir. It was very exciting, and the meal was tasty too!' Tan chuckled. He was a good lad.

'Are you willing to do the same thing again?' I asked.

After a little thought he answered. 'Yes Sir, but I'm not too keen on returning to that house.'

'Don't worry, Tan, next time it will be outside, not inside!'

Two days later the platoon was flogging its way through the jungle to the west of Sun Tian Kang, heading for an old CT camp which we had used on several occasions as our own base when we were in the area. Whenever we did, I always used to examine a particular tree for it had a certain morbid interest for me. It was while we were attacking the camp, and I was firing from the cover of this particular tree, that the bark by my shoulder started to splinter. I dropped to the ground and turning my head saw a maniac blasting away with his sten-gun right behind me. It was one of my own men. Slowly the bullet marks were healing; soon nature would have done her work and the evidence would have disappeared.

By late afternoon, *bashas* had been erected and food was being prepared. Somehow Jo-Jo would produce something tasty. As the brief twilight faded, Shaffie and I would discuss the plans for the next day. Then, perhaps, the conversation would range more widely, and he would talk about his life. Shaffie preferred the excitement of the jungle to being a mere cop on a city beat, and not only because of the lure of danger money, though this was a big attraction to tempt men into a jungle company and on to the 'jungle beat'.

The platoon was made up of Malays, Chinese, Indians and Eurasians: they were Moslem, Hindu, Buddhist and Christian. Yet this mixture of nationalities and religions made no difference. Their united aim was to rid their country of Communism. During these twilight talks over the years I was told over and over again how ruthlessly the Communists murdered innocent victims. I heard first-hand accounts of police stations being burned down with women and children trapped inside; of convoys attacked on lonely jungle roads and the wounded thrown into blazing vehicles. The more I learnt of the enemy, the more I, too, came to hate them.

Next morning Shaffie departed northwards with one section, while I set off south with section two. The third section would stay at base guarding and preparing food for our return. I had slept well but was feeling below par - nothing, I thought, that a patrol wouldn't cure.

The jungle here was clean, without much undergrowth to hold you back. It proved an easy march, peaceful and quiet, which suited me, given the way I was feeling. I quickly woke up, however, when I found a freshly used track. We followed it until it reached a stream. The footprints, which were quite clear in the soft mud, went into the water, but then on the other side the footprints also went into the water. Both sets went in and none came out! A couple of years ago I would have been puzzled by this, but now, being jungle-wise, I knew the answer. The CTs would walk into a stream normally, then turn round in midstream and walk out backwards, in order to confuse anyone who might be tracking them.

'Clever bastards,' I thought, 'they know all the jungle tricks.'

On the far side of the stream, we followed the footprints that appeared to be leading to it, and, as I had expected, after a few yards they changed direction. Our quarry had turned and was now walking normally. We scrutinised the area around us. There were several stumps of saplings; obviously they had taken the lengths for building their *bashas*. A track led away through the bush. Very gingerly, we followed it. By this time I was feeling really ill, but took my turn as leading tracker, as I did not want the men to think I was trying to dodge it. For obvious reasons, it was the most dangerous position.

On we went, crouching, straining our ears for any noise, sniffing the air for smells. We stopped and paused for several minutes; nothing but a green shadowy twilight which held us spellbound. No talking; any communication was done by sign language. We moved on. With each step I placed my feet down with the utmost care, trying to make no noise. I was tracking stealthily forward in this manner when suddenly something curled round and gripped my ankle! Before I knew what was happening, I was up-ended, hoisted by my ankle, until I was hanging upside down like a pendulum. The yell I let out must have been heard for miles! Quickly the men cut me down, and then we began to see the funny side of it. For all my care and cunning, I had walked into one of the native game traps. These are simple, but extremely effective - as I had discovered for myself. A strong sapling is bent over until it is under great tension, and then held in position by a wire. This acts as a snare, and, as soon as anything is caught, the sapling is tripped and whips the victim into the air.

Thirty yards from the trap we found their camp. It had been evacuated several hours earlier. There were only three *bashas*: two had been in use recently, but the third was a spare. More than likely it was a staging camp for couriers, with a permanent staff of four or five. The couriers on their long journeys would spend perhaps a couple of days here to recuperate and collect documents for delivery to Communist organisations elsewhere in Malaya.

As it was lunchtime, we halted in the camp. Lunch was the usual cold rice and dried fish, but I did not touch my food; I slept instead. By now I was feeling really ill, and my body had large itchy lumps all over it. To extend my rest I decided to lay an ambush outside the camp for a couple of hours. We soon settled down. I could feel the hot sun on my body, and it made me feel a little better, but the reddish lumps were still irritating and getting worse.

Corporal Lattif was on the bren-gun next to me. The afternoon dragged on. I checked my watch and whispered to him that in fifteen minutes we would pull out. At that moment his brow furrowed in concentration. He tapped his ear with his forefinger to indicate that he had heard a movement. I listened intently; a slow crunching sound was coming our way. There was nothing to be seen only the endless green encircling gloom. The movement had ceased; tranquillity returned. For several minutes we sweated it out, rooted in our positions, wondering if 'they' had sensed us. Then the crunching movement started again. Closer and closer it came, very slowly, very deliberately. All our weapons were aimed in its direction. The tension was unbearable and I was on the verge of giving the order to open fire, when 'they' appeared - in all its glory, a full-grown tiger! Still in the same deliberate way it headed towards us, sniffing us out, closer and closer, so close I could smell the earthy scent of it; I could almost have touched it. I could easily have shot it, but we weren't on a tiger shoot. Suddenly it halted, alert, suspicious, superb. I was too fascinated to be frightened, even. Perhaps one of us moved, for it let out a roar then turned and loped away. I must admit that we all gave a sigh of relief as the sound died away in the distance.

I called the ambush off and headed back to base camp. I was feeling so wretched I handed over to Corporal Lattif to get us safely back to base. It was all I could do to stagger along with my head bowed. Every now and then I lurched into thorny undergrowth, lacerating my arms and face.

As soon as we reached camp I struggled out of my sopping green rags of a uniform and into my PT shorts. I did not bathe in the stream, or even de-leech myself; I couldn't. I simply scrambled under my poncho, covered myself with my lightweight, damp blanket and tried to sleep. Shaffie and Jo-Jo examined me. Shaffie collected all the salt from the men and rubbed it on my body while Jo-Jo concocted one of his herbal remedies which tasted absolutely revolting. I just about managed to swallow it and keep it down. A couple of the men who were familiar with jungle illnesses diagnosed it as perhaps having been caused by the pollen of *Poko Rengis* (Rengis tree) which affects the skin in this way. Or it might have been the secretion from a particular species of caterpillar or a giant millipede crawling over me as I slept on the jungle floor, for the ground teemed with insect life in infinite variety.

On several occasions I woke in the night to find legions of ants scurrying through my *basha*. Once I had foolishly left my jungle boots strewn on the ground instead of hanging them up, and by the following morning they had been taken over by ants who had built a nest in them. I have been stung by a small scorpion which had sought sanctuary in my uniform, and by hornets. Hornet stings are very painful and make you feel under the weather. Some joker thought a climbing frog must have pissed on the *Tuan*; their urine is considered highly dangerous.

Whatever it was, the *Poko Rengis*, a caterpillar, an millipede, a urinating frog or something else equally unpleasant, I was sick. I lay under my damp blanket shaking, near delirious. Jo-Jo fussed around and did his best to help me. During that night it rained heavily and, with the thunder and lightning, the jungle seemed to explode around me and intensify my delirium. The men had mustered a couple of extra blankets for me, which did help to keep me warm during the night. In the morning Jo-Jo shoved a mug of hot sweet tea into my hand. I was pleased to find that all the swellings had gone and my headache was not as severe, but I still felt weak. I crawled from under my poncho and found a place in the sun.

Shaffie came to inform me that two sections had left two hours previously, one to patrol east and the other west. After a bathe in the river I felt much better. Jo-Jo knocked up some food which I wolfed down, and, while I was eating, a light shower fell. The Malays have a saying: 'Hot rain - be on guard - blood will flow.' This proverb has been quoted to me many many times, and now I was to hear it yet again. After a few warm spots had fallen, Ramli was there.

'*Tuan hujan panas, jaga darah mesti jatoh*'.

'Thank you for warning me Ramli,' I said, and slipped back under my poncho.

I had just started to doze off when I heard gunfire. Or had I? Shaffie was soon beside me with confirmation. He had taken a compass bearing; the firing was coming from Corporal Lattif's section, to the east. We heard it again and this time I could distinguish the thudding sound of the bren-gun from the crack of the carbines. Quite a little skirmish was taking place.

After a while the usual eerie silence settled back once more. Trying to measure distance by noise in the jungle is almost impossible, for hills and other natural features create echoes and distort the sound. Almost three hours had elapsed since the sections had left for their respective areas. Corporal Ayob's lot, patrolling to the west, should return first; Lattif's, if they'd been in action, would probably take longer to make their way back. We did not have long to wait. One of the sentries gave the alert and we took up defensive positions until we had positively identified our own men returning. Corporal Ayob soon emerged, leading his section into base.

On setting eyes on me he said, 'Good to see you looking much better, *Tuan'*.

'Thank you Corporal Ayob. Did you hear any firing, Corporal? I enquired.

'Firing, *Tuan*? We heard nothing at all!'

Moreover, they had found no sign of CTs.

'All we saw was a large herd of wild boar, a python and a few monkeys. Shall I go and look for Lattif's section?'

Corporal Ayob was a highly experienced jungle type with many years' service and an excellent combat record. He could always be relied upon to volunteer if there was an emergency. In this case, though, he agreed with Shaffie and me that it might be a bit dicey to go to Corporal Lattif's assistance; they would be nervous and trigger-happy after their engagement. I could not risk a confrontation between two of my sections.

I checked the time; in an hour it would be dark, and there would be no question of going out to search for them. We had an old trick if a section was lost; sometimes it might be only a hundred yards away but unable to locate the camp. I would fire one shot into the air and wait for an answering shot. When it came, we would take a compass bearing on them. After a few seconds we would fire again, so that they could take a compass bearing on that. Fifteen seconds was the prearranged interval between shots. Shaffie stood by me with his prismatic compass, ready to take a bearing. I fired one shot into the darkening sky. The sweep hand of my watch slowly moved through its ninety degree arc.

'Fifteen seconds gone, Shaffie.'

No answering shot came. Seventeen, eighteen, nineteen, then after exactly twenty seconds, we heard the report of a rifle shot. It did not sound very far away.

'Lattif's five seconds late!' I said to Shaffie.

'I've fixed them at south-east, *Tuan*!'

'Good Shaffie.'

I waited the fifteen seconds and fired again. Twenty minutes later they arrived, carrying a dead CT trussed to a pole. While Lattif set about his rice, he told me of the day's events. They had spotted a Communist camp on the opposite side of the valley. They slithered and scrambled down the steep side of the hill and across the river at the bottom. As they made their way up the equally steep and slippery slope on the other side, they were seen and fired upon. They at once fired back. The CTs had a tactical advantage for they were able to fire down on the section, but for some unknown reason they broke off the engagement and fled.

When Lattif and his men reached the camp, which had accommodation for six to eight, they found one dead terrorist who had been killed during the firing. Their progress had been slowed down because of having to carry the body and having become disorientated, Lattif had been relieved to hear my shot. They also brought disturbing news: they had seen fresh tracks not far from our camp. If there were terrorists that close, it would be as well to be on guard, and I laid simple booby traps round the camp perimeter. These consisted of empty cigarette tins, the round type which hold fifty, in which was placed a hand-grenade with the pin withdrawn. The tin holds the arm down position, so the grenade is still safe, but once the tin is knocked over the grenade falls out and explodes. Shaffie and I set four of these traps around the camp. At the back of our minds was always the thought that some marauding nocturnal beast might trip one of them. In the morning the two of us would recover the grenades and replace the pins, a job I never relished.

Darkness had fallen by the time we'd placed the last trap, so I ordered stand-by and went round to each *basha* to have a few words with the men.

I told Tan that he might be called upon to do his 'act' the next day, for I had worked out a scheme. Ramli, who was sharing the *basha* with Tan and had predicted bloodshed with warm rain, was overjoyed.

'*Tuan*,' he crowed, 'I was right about the *Hujan panas*!'

'Yes Ramli,' I said, 'you were'.

In the jungle superstitions like this were somehow less easy to dismiss than they were over the bar in the mess.

Before going to sleep that night I took three M & B tablets (a sort of paracetamol, quinine / analgesic tablet that helps to combat fever). I might have wished that the trussed-up corpse had not been lying quite so close to my *basha* but, corpse or no corpse, I was soon fast asleep.

Early dawn saw me up and about and feeling completely recovered. Was it Jo-Jo's brew or the M & B? I had not yet examined the corpse, so I took this opportunity to remove the documents from his pockets. I don't know why, but I always felt guilty doing this, as if I were a thief or a looter. I noticed, by the light-coloured ribbon of skin around his wrist, that he had usually worn a watch and presumed that someone had taken it. Judging by the size of the camp and its position, not too deep in the jungle, my guess was that he was a branch committee member for Sun Tian Kang and the surrounding areas. This gave me an idea. There was a rubber plantation not very far beyond the camp which Lattif's section had attacked, and the tappers on it must have heard the firing. In which case the chances were, first, that they were hand in glove with the Communists and, second, the action might give me an opportunity to confirm my suspicions.

With this in mind, I got PC Tan to dress, once again, in Communist uniform. He had a bit of difficulty tying the dead man's puttees neatly, but we finally made him reasonably respectable. With a red-star hat perched on his head, he looked every inch the part. His story this time was that his camp had been attacked the day before, he had lost contact with the other members, and could they help him?

71

A brisk trek soon brought us to the jungle fringe. By examining the rubber trees we could tell that tapping was taking place and therefore we knew that the coolies would be returning to collect the milky white latex dripping into the cups attached to the trees. In fact, there was a tapper at work making the incisions in the bark and fastening the cups in position and so we pulled back out of sight on the jungle edge. We did not have to wait long. Shaffie pointed out a couple of tappers who were doing their rounds and heading towards us. This was the moment for Tan to move into the estate. From our position we were able to keep him in sight. When the tappers saw him they showed no alarm. Tan lit up a cigarette and gesticulated in the direction of the jungle. He spent about ten minutes talking to them and then re-joined us.

On his return, we moved further into the jungle, where we could talk unheard and unseen. Tan told us that the tappers had heard the shooting and would help him. It appeared that they were members of the 'Min Yuen', the Communist fifth-column organisation. They had the reputation of being able to arrange anything. Tan had arranged another rendezvous with them for the following day.

On our way back to the camp we were assailed by an appalling stench and we soon came to its source. Round a bend in the river there were literally thousands of dead fish floating, with millions of flies buzzing amongst them, and more and more drifting down the river to join the carnage. Thirty yards down the stream was a sluice-way made out of branches and here the fish had piled up. We ripped it away and the dead fish were slowly carried along by the current downstream. The Communists had poisoned the river.

'All this for a few fish,' I said to Shaffie; 'the waste!'

'Yes Tuan, they could have caught enough fish for their needs with hook and line and left no tell-tale evidence behind.'

On several occasions I have been perplexed by the Communists' attitude. On the one hand they could display extreme guile, trickery and jungle-craft; and on the other, they could do something as clumsy and idiotic as this. However, if after two years in the jungle, I felt able to criticise them, I was well aware that it would be dangerous ever to underestimate them, or become over-confident.

We left the stink of dead fish behind and in two hours were back at our base camp. What a relief, then, to bathe in the river and remove the leeches with which I was covered. I never wore underpants or vest on operations; they would have been soaked in blood and simply been something else to wash out. I did not wear socks either for the same reason. Shaving was out of the question, though I did hear of a British Army unit that shaved every day on operations. They must have had some cushy base camp! We carried extra food instead. Apart from anything else, men freshly washed and smelling of aftershave would immediately give away an ambush position, however well concealed, to an experienced CT. Tan, for his next role, would not even use soap during his morning wash.

Jo-Jo announced that my meal was ready: rice and fresh fish. I gulped and thought of that rotting mass we'd passed; but Jo-Jo had caught this fish in the nearby river, and it was delicious. So much for our simple domestic lives when we were on patrol.

Next day we would be returning to HQ. I had not given the Min Yuen at the rubber estate much time to contact the fighting units of the Communists but, with this particular area being a hotbed, they might well have made contact within a couple of hours. There was one possible flaw in the plan. If the unit from the camp which Lattif had attacked returned there and found that their dead comrade had mysteriously disappeared, they would guess that there were Security Forces in the area an act accordingly. I could only hope that they hadn't discovered the missing body and go ahead as arranged.

We broke camp very early the following morning. The corpse proved a problem, and some patrols in deep jungle had been known to bring only the head back for identification. One patrol leader carried a head about for some days through jungle and swamp, and inevitably it soon began to decay. When he got back to HQ he marched into the administration officer and dumped the disgusting object on the desk for identification! Not long afterwards orders came from the highest level that this practice was to be halted, so we had to carry our burden with us.

We reached the jungle edge before the tappers arrived. They cannot work in rain as it affects the bleeding of the latex; but the sky was clear of rain-clouds that morning. We hoped for the best.

After half an hour or so the coolies turned up, the women distinctive in their large conical hats. We kept them under surveillance because the coolies keep to their own area of work every day and we knew that the men Tan spoke to yesterday would soon be cutting away with their specially designed knives at the trees close to us. After fifteen minutes Tan whispered that the man moving along the nearby lines of trees was one of them. I patted Tan on the shoulder and whispered to him to be careful, and he left cover and ambled towards him. The tapper offered him a cigarette. Tan's instructions were to keep as close to the man as possible; he was safe then if he was being set up, because CTs would not open fire on one of their own members of the Min Yuen.

Tan was a natural at this game. He even fumbled over taking a light for his cigarette in order to keep close. He spent several minutes with the man, and returned to our jungle lair to report. The Min Yuen had apparently contacted their local armed unit, and they would be in the area later that morning. More than likely they were here already, less than a hundred yards away, watching and listening just as we were.

We idled away a couple of hours, keeping the rubber estate under observation all the time, and being constantly attacked by mosquitoes and beset by flies. The presence of the corpse didn't help. It was impossible not to be aware of it, and I even saw a vividly coloured butterfly exploring the lips. It was only then that I noticed the man had a fine set of gold teeth. At that moment a couple of shots were fired, quite close by, but out of our line of vision.

What did it mean? Had the local armed unit arrived, realised that it was a trap and started to massacre the tappers? That wouldn't be out of character if they suspected the coolies of double-crossing them. The only thing to do was to find out quickly.

With a few men, Shaffie and I made our way into the estate. As we reached the jungle edge, another shot rang out. Amongst the rubber trees there was a group of people, some of them tappers; were the others CTs? We could not shoot for fear of hitting the coolies, even if we'd been sure. When they saw us they quickly dispersed. We dashed across to where they had gathered. There we saw the cause of the commotion: not terrorists or their victims but a four-foot monitor lizard. That was that, my carefully laid plan had been sabotaged - by a lizard!

Although we tried questioning the men and women working on the estate, all we got was that now familiar hard, blank stony stare: shots? what shots? monitor? what monitor? You'd have thought they were all deaf, dumb and blind.

We were pretty careful, though, as we headed back to base through the estate and along the two-mile jungle track that led to the road. This was ideal ambushing country, and a famous highland regiment had suffered heavy casualties when they were caught on this very track. At the danger spots, I would send a squad round the rear to make sure all was clear. We had no food left, so our packs were light, but we still had to lug our fly-blown friend along with us.

Once on the road, I flagged down the first vehicle. It happened to be carrying a load of pineapples. The driver agreed to take four men the six miles into Cha'ah, where they would arrange for transport and an armoured escort to come and collect us. While we waited, we did justice to the pineapples which the driver had left us. That somehow summed up the contradictions of the job we were doing: leeches, being made ill by being pissed on by frogs, blank-faced coolies, a dead lizard, and squatting by the roadside eating pineapples in the company of a corpse now definitely past its best, and whose presence provided the justification for the whole exercise.

six

brotherly love - and a nasty headache

While I was away, a senior Communist from the local area had surrendered and was busy betraying his former comrades - including his own brother - for money. This unpleasant character, with the name Lam, volunteered to take me to a track which was often used by the CT group to which his brother belonged: so, within forty eight hours of my getting back from the previous operation, I was off again with a section of men and our fratricidal chum.

We set up our base camp just off the Singapore-Kuala Lumpur railway line - a spot, according to Lam, only two hundred yards from the CTs' route. It wasn't an ideal site, as the only water supply was a trickle of a stream, but it would have to do. Once settled, I set off to reconnoitre. It was obvious from the number of fresh footprints that the track was well used, and I was glad we had reached it late in the afternoon, and so had time to pick our ambush position and killing zone.

Lam told me that the people who had used it were probably members of the North Johore Political Bureau and their bodyguards.

'When will they be back?' I asked.

No answer; just a shrug and a cold smile made somehow deadlier by an array of gold teeth.

'You didn't tell me that other units besides your brother's came this way?'

No answer, just that same chilling grin.

'If your brother's lot have joined up with the North Johore Politburo,' I said, 'we're in for it.'

There were only six of us, whereas there could be a dozen or more of them; but Lam - when he deigned to answer - was quite definite that the NJP would have been going back to their camp and would not be returning this way. I hoped he knew what he was talking about. What I didn't know, and Lam didn't tell me, was that the NJP's headquarters were less than half a mile away, in the jungle on the other side of the railway line. I was led to it three weeks later by another informer, but by then the birds had flown.

We settled down to wait. I hoped we wouldn't be waiting too long: if there was no rain, the stream would dry up, and we should be in trouble. Quite apart from thirst, the Moslems use water to wipe their bums, and I had enough problems without a constipated section on my hands! To anxieties over the water supply was added another - the need for absolute silence. We were so close to our ambush position the least sound might give us away. I wasn't at all happy about the operation as a whole, and I didn't like Lam.

At eight o'clock the following morning we were in position with the track covered. Lam had told me how many men were likely to be in the party, what arms they would be carrying and which direction they would be coming from, and we were all ready for them. But it is extremely difficult, especially in the bush with the heat, flies, mosquitoes and creepy-crawlies, to remain still and alert, hour after hour. When by four o'clock in the afternoon nothing had happened, I called it a day and took the section back to camp - which wasn't all that much of an improvement.

The next day the same thing happened - or rather, didn't - and I was becoming more and more dubious. Had news of Lam's defection reached his brother's unit and made them decide to lie low? I put this to him, but he would have none of it.

'No one knows about it yet,' he said with his golden smile. Cunning bastard. Like so many of his kind, he had served with the MPAJA during the war, and when it was over had joined the MPLA, until greed had overcome ideology. But that didn't explain why he was prepared to murder his own brother - or perhaps it did. By proving himself utterly ruthless towards his ex-comrades, he hoped to increase his value in the eyes of the Security Forces and so be paid a higher rate. I found his cynicism so sickening that I even suggested that he could stay in camp and take no part in the ambush, but he turned the offer down. He wanted, so he said, to be in at the kill.

Next morning we were back once more in our ambush positions. I had made one or two changes. I had put Lam with one of the old hands on the right flank, where they would be the first to see the enemy, and had put a new man, who was on his first ambush, by my side so that I could restrain him if he became over-excited. Shaffie, the ever-reliable, and one man on my left were armed with a sten and a carbine; Lam and his chap had that deadliest of close-range weapons, a sawn-off shotgun. The whole position stretched for only eight yards.

In an ambush, discipline is everything. Normally no one fires until I give the order; the only exception to this rule is if one of the section sees the enemy behaving as if they suspect something. Then on his own initiative he shoots to kill. We settled into our positions to wait. I sensed that today was going to be the day. Silent, unmoving, we crouched within the cover of the jungle. The flies buzzed around our faces; sweat trickled down our bodies. God, what wouldn't I have given for a bath and a long cold beer! On operations our ablutions rarely extended beyond a quick sluice in the stream, though I insisted on cleaning my teeth wherever we were.

My nerves, stretched taut, tweaked me sharply back to the present. There was a sound that wasn't one of the usual jungle sounds; footsteps softly padding along the track towards us. I nodded to Shaffie and eased the safety-catch off the carbine. They did not know it, but we were ready for them. Lam and his partner were out of my view; they must soon see them approaching. Then, like a high-voltage shock, came one single shot, followed a second later by the stutter of a sten from Lam's position.

Shaffie and I burst out of cover in time to see a number of figures racing away in the direction of the tracks. We belted after them, firing as we ran. By the time we reached the line, the last of them was just disappearing into the jungle on the far side. Although we followed them for a bit, I knew it was hopeless; as well try and find a friend in a football crowd. They'd been warned and they'd got clean away. I was livid, and went straight up to Lam and jammed my carbine into his stomach.

'You fired that shot deliberately,' I said

'No, *Tuan*, I swear. They saw me.'

'You're lying. How many CTs were there?'

'Six or seven.'

'Was your brother among them?'

'Yes.'

'So you fired to warn him. When it came to the point, you couldn't do it!'

'No, *Tuan*. They saw me. That's why I fired.'

Just then a train came roaring past, which stopped me telling him what I thought of him. When it had passed, I noticed for the first time that the safety-catch on the carbine was still set to fire. That was his lucky day.

Back at camp, Shaffie and I mulled the matter over, but neither of us could think of any reason for that single shot other than to warn his brother.

'If it hadn't been for that,' Shaffie said despondently, 'we'd have got five of them, *Tuan*. I'm certain of it!'

'So am I,' I said.

With that exasperating thought, we broke camp and headed back for HQ at Cha'ah. I made sure that Lam walked ahead of me: I wasn't taking any chances. Later I heard from Special Branch that Lam's girlfriend was with the party at the ambush and that was why he blew it.

As if the turncoat Lam wasn't enough, it was immediately after this I got lumbered with Inspector Chan of the city CID. The company commander introduced us. I was to take him out on a short operation, five or six days, to give him a taste of the jungle.

'Don't go too fast, Roy. Remember this is his first jungle patrol.'

'Right Sir,' I said. 'Which part of the woods are we heading for?'

'They say the bluebells are pretty round Bekok,' he said, 'so you'd better go and admire them. As you know, Goh Peng attacked Paloh police post yesterday; he's the man you're after.'

We had fourty eight hours before we were due to set off, and I made the most of the bath and the beer, I can tell you. I also briefed Inspector Chan on our forthcoming operation, but he didn't display much curiosity or enthusiasm. I gained the distinct impression that Inspector Chan wasn't looking forward to his jungle baptism. Well, we should see. It was to be quite a big patrol; Chan and I had fifteen men each from our platoons - enough to deal with Goh Peng if we were lucky enough to come across him. We boarded our transport early on Sunday morning and headed for Bekok village and the Kempas rubber estate beyond. There we de-bussed and entered the 'bluebell wood', alias the same old suffocating, steamy jungle. What follows is taken from notes I made at the time.

day one

Found a decent spot to make base camp, position MR/065295. Some joker has introduced a coding system for position reports, based on a key word. Ours this time is KENILWORTH = 1234567890. So we're at HWL-ETL. Hope the bugger enjoys playing with his bloody little pins on his office map when he's sorted it out. Sooner or later, as Harry Barlow remarked, it's going to lead to an unholy balls-up. In plain language, we've come across an abandoned CT camp, probably for ten people, and evacuated at a guess a week or so ago. Position 045291, or, in fancy language, HIL-ETK. A plague on all desk wallahs! A plague on all radios that play up or pack up, too![5]

Appendix 'B' to
HQ MALAYA Air
Instruction No. 9

GROUND/AIR PANEL CODE

SIGNAL   **MEANING**

H   1. S.O.S. - Ground Party lost and in
            need of positional fix.

H̲   2. Ground party in need of supply drop
            (food and medical supplies)

H̳   3. Ground party has suffered casualties
            and in need of assistance.
            (supply drop and ground help)

W   4. Require wireless set

WI   5. Require wireless battery

W̲   6. Require wireless set and battery

Λ̳   7. Ground party in action with enemy in
            direction of arrow and in need of air
            support. (All own troops behind
            the arrowhead, and horizontal bars
            denote distance of enemy, one bar
            for each 100 yards.

▢   8. Require small arms ammunition

⊠   9. Cancel airstrike or supply drop not
            required

L   10. Helicopter required for casualty
             evacuation. (Signal to be dis-
             played at best touch-down for
             helicopter).

.

What the devil's up with Chan? He's behaving like a wet weekend in Wigan. A lot of use he's going to be if we have a dust-up.

Tackled Chan. At first, he said nothing; then, cool as you like, he explained.

'My religion (I gather he's a Buddhist) forbids me to kill. If we contact any CTs, I shall not be able to shoot.'

I was dumbfounded.

'Well, what the hell are you doing here then?'

No answer, then, 'I do not like the jungle. Tomorrow I shall return to HQ with my men.'

What do you know? I've tried everything. I've humoured him, cursed him, insulted him; nothing has any effect. I accused him of cowardice or desertion; I told him it would be the end of his police career - I'll make certain of that - and I might as well have been talking to a tree.

'Besides,' he said, 'I have a headache!'

That really did it! I lost my temper. I told him I'd spent two years fighting Communism in his country - not my country, **his** - and now, to have your joint leader decide to walk out on you in the middle of an operation which had a good chance of success ....well, I was disgusted with him. It all got pretty heated and made no difference at all. He says he'll leave in the morning. Good riddance!

day two

Tried again this morning. Even the fact that some of Chan's men have been coming to Shaffie and asking to stay hasn't altered Chan's mind.

'Take a note of their names,' I said, 'I'll see they don't suffer guilt by association.'

As for Chan himself, before he left, I took him on one side, out of hearing of his men, and told him to his face he was a coward.

'And if you get lost - and you probably will - don't try and return to find me, or you'll risk getting shot.'

'But I'm wearing green uniform, not khaki,' he said.

'Goh Peng got away with jungle-greens from Paloh, and weapons as well, I said. I added, just to put the wind up him, 'Don't cross grid lines thirty and ten, or the Gurkhas will get you!'

With that I told him to fuck off - and that's what he's done.

Wish I had Harry with me. I remember that time we were on a six-day patrol together and we followed tracks for six or eight hours and they petered out on hard ground, just like that. We couldn't agree which way they'd gone and he went one way and I another.

'If you get back to HQ first,' were his parting words, 'fill the fridge with beer!'

Four days later I was back first. I did put the beer in the fridge and he turned up a few minutes later. For some reason, this made me liable to pay for it. Good old Harry, and bloody Chan!'

Broke camp and headed south-east. Came across another deserted basha. Nothing there, so pressed on. Had a nasty scare when one of the scouts pointed out a twenty foot python right across the track. I hate snakes, all snakes, especially the ones that hang down like thin green branches and you feel that clammy 'thing' on the back of your neck - ugh! They're not supposed to have rattlesnakes here, but they've got something very like them. The men call them 'elor', and we came across three of them on one occasion, rattling away like a box of dice. I didn't hang about.

later:

Made camp near the river; a good spot, I reckon, but the men don't like it. I was squatting, cleaning my carbine, when an agitated Shaffie dashed up.

'Tuan!'

'What's the matter?'

'The men - its not like them at all. They say there are 'hantus', Tuan.'

'Hantus?' I said, 'Ghosts, eh? Nonsense.'

'Aziz and Harun have seen it, Tuan, over there, by that twisted tree!'

Ghosts - pah! I don't believe in ghosts, and even if I did its my duty to stay cool and detached. Yet I felt a cold shiver running up and down my spine. Yes, maybe there **was** something odd about that tree, something a bit, well, haunted.

Imagination started to go berserk as darkness fell, and in the light of the moon through the branches, I could make out four or five little knots of men, huddled together as if waiting - for what? I suddenly remembered Chan's departure: pity the bastard wasn't around; this would have cured his headache.

The moon went in; it was like a door closing. The jungle was black. We couldn't move; I wished we could. 'Hantus' or no 'hantus', there was something evil and eerie about that place. No question about it. A movement. Involuntarily I started; but it was *only Shaffie. Truth be told, I was glad of his company.*

'They've seen it again, Tuan!'

'It's only an orang-utan,' I said, with little conviction.

'No, Tuan. It's no an orang-utan. It's a 'hantu'.' He paused.

'Aziz knows about these things. He says 'hantu' has come to watch us because we have violated his sanctuary. We must leave at first light.'

'Do you believe him, Shaffie?' I found I was whispering; we both were.

'Yes, Tuan.'

'All right. Tell the men to be ready to move at dawn.'

After he'd gone, I sat for a bit. Strange, there's none of the usual cacophony you get in the jungle at night. What's that? A breeze has sprung up; that moaning? The wind stirring the trees, what else? It's getting on my nerves. Might as well turn in and try and ignore it.

day three

I woke up choking for breath. I'd pulled the blanket over my head. It was still dark, and deathly quiet except for that moaning sound. Stupid to be scared. Of what? But I was, shit-scared. I must have dropped off again, all the same, because the next I knew was hearing the ever-faithful Jo-Jo struggling to kindle a fire by my basha. It wasn't quite dawn, but the bashas were all down, and there were several fires winking away, and the men were heating up their rice for breakfast.

Shaffie came over. Apparently I was the only one to have

had any sleep: the men hadn't even tried to sleep, but had sat up all night while the 'hantus' prowled round, putting the fear of God into them. Most of them, I discovered, had seen or heard it.

'Was the Tuan afraid of the 'hantus'?' Aziz asked.

I admitted I had been; it was the worst night I'd ever spent in the jungle.

'So,' Aziz said, 'if the Tuan was afraid of the 'hantus', he must believe in them.'

'I don't know,' I said; 'but I certainly caught your fear. Fear spreads like a contagion.'

I can't say that that convinced either Aziz or me. There was something supernatural about last night, something far stronger than the men's terror. Whatever it was, I can do without a repetition. I've never seen the men tidy up a camp-site so painstakingly as they did this morning - 'to keep the 'hantus' happy,' they said. Good idea, I thought.

We left as soon as we could, South East still, until we reached the Quek Shin rubber estate. It was deserted; the tappers had already finished for the day. We pulled back out of the open, sunlit avenues of rubber trees and melted once more into the green gloom and found this camp-site. Shaffie smiled when I suggested quite seriously that we'd better check it for 'hantus' as well as CTs. But this is quite different; none of that aura, that sense of being watched that we had last night. The men are quite at ease, back to their usual bantering. That means they're happy here.

day five

We've been keeping out of sight, watching the unsuspecting tappers as they go about their business, hoping Goh Peng will fall into our ambush, but no such luck, and now we're just about out of rations. Time to set off back. What a trip! What a week! First Lam, then Inspector bloody Chan, then 'hantus' and at the end of it all, nothing. That's jungle-bashing for you.

And that was about it. We got a lot of hostile stares as we headed through the rubber estate to the police station in Paloh village which was none the worse for the raid the previous week, though the station sergeant was pretty shaken, and one of his men had been wounded. There, the armoured vehicles picked us up and took us to Yong Peng. Every time I'd been to that village I'd felt uneasy, and this time was not exception. The place was such a Communist hotbed, I always half-expected to find the red flag flying over it. It was a relief to be safely inside its heavily fortified police station.

The fifteen miles from Yong Peng were a favourite haunt of Goh Peng Tuan's for ambushes, and we took no chances: the brens were manned, with safety-catches off, the whole way. It was almost curfew time as we sped along, and we saw no other vehicles.

Everyone's always glad to see a patrol safely back from a mission; especially when they've not been in radio contact with HQ. During the five or more days that they're 'missing' anything could have happened. I duly reported to the OC. There was no sign of Inspector Chan, and I asked where he was.

'I sent him and his platoon to Kulai on guard duties,' he said

in a neutral voice, 'to save you embarrassment.'

'Good of you, Sir,' I said in a similar voice.

That was all that was said. I put in my report, and he got away with a sharp rap over the knuckles from the Police Department. He was lucky; if he'd been a British officer he'd have been dismissed and put on the first plane back to the UK. I didn't see Chan again while I was stationed in Johore, but our paths crossed, many months later, among the jungle-clad mountains on the Perak-Kalantan border - as will be related in due course.

# seven

fiascos 1 and 2

'*Tuan! Tuan!*'

Jo-Jo's croaky voice forcing its way into my sleeping brain.

'*Tuan! Tuan!*'

There was no escaping it.

I glanced at the clock: eleven o'clock mid-morning. But I'd been out on a night ambush and had only got back, soaked to the skin, after dark. Three hours' sleep and here was Jo-Jo with his '*Tuan! Tuan!*'

'What is it, Jo-Jo?' I demanded peevishly.

'The OC wants to see you straight away. Very important, he says.'

'Oh God!' I hauled myself out of bed and into my uniform and went over to the mess in not a very pleasant frame of mind. What had they got lined up for me this time?

With the OC were two men I didn't know, one from Special Branch, the other an officer from the Gurkha Battalion whose operational area was next to ours. The introductions over, the Special Branch chap explained why, among other things, I had been dragged out of bed. It seemed that a member of the North Johore Politburo (NJP) by the name of Chen had defected the day before, and was prepared to guide a patrol to their HQ, which was in the Gurkha's area, not ours.

At first the SB hadn't believed it; it was too good to be true that a man of his rank in the party should have surrendered. Consequently, Chen was treated initially with considerable suspicion. However, Chen had set things up very cleverly. Apparently he had led a section of his men, including his own bodyguard, to one of the rubber estates with the ostensible object of haranguing the workers and, if the opportunity arose, of laying an ambush for the Security Forces. He carried out the first part with only his bodyguard with him, leaving the rest in the jungle. Then, on his way to rejoin them, he pretended that he'd heard English voices, told the section that the SF were about, and sent them back to HQ in twos and threes while he and his bodyguard remained. As soon as they'd gone, he murdered the bodyguard and gave himself up.

By doing it this way, he had not only covered himself, but had increased his chances of a reward by presenting the SF with a corpse, and with his own and his ex-bodyguard's weapons, which also guaranteed his bona fides. In addition, it would be some days before those at NJP headquarters began to suspect that something was amiss.

This was all excellent. The only snag was that Chen refused to guide the SF unless he had a European Police Officer with him to ensure his safety. And this, I now learnt, was to be me.

'So, Roy,' the OC said, 'you've to wet-nurse Chen, and, as you know the area, act as a liaison between him and the Gurkha platoon commander. It's their show, though, remember. You're there simply to look after Chen and act as link-man with the Gurkhas.'

'Fine,' I said. 'When do we start?'

'First light tomorrow. Now get yourself to Segamat as fast as you can, and the Gurkhas'll brief you.'

Two hours later I was in the Segamat Ops room with a packed rucksack, and was being put in the picture by the Gurkhas' CO.

It wouldn't be true to say that I had forebodings, but I quickly saw that there were going to be problems. In the first place, the platoon commander spoke very little English, and my Gurkha was nil, so it wasn't easy to put over the finer points of the operation to each other. He was a fine, tough little man who, like all the Gurkhas, smiled a lot, but that didn't entirely solve the language difficulty.

Next, I was introduced to Chen. Having recently had a bellyful of another SEP (namely Lam), I wasn't actually in love with these bastards, useful though they sometimes were, and Chen seemed true to type. Short, pock-marked, thin as a bean-pole, with a handshake like a dead fish, and dressed in a new shirt and slacks, he might have been mistaken at first sight for a junior clerk. Then I noticed his ankles; he wasn't wearing socks, and they were covered in the scars of leech-bites. No, he wasn't a clerk, not with those. Also, he was wearing a large, obviously expensive gold-plated watch which looked grotesque on his thin wrist - part of the spoils of treachery, I guessed, though how he'd had the time to buy it I couldn't imagine. Perhaps it had belonged to his late bodyguard. He was chain-smoking, obviously extremely nervous, and when he smiled there was something slick and cold about it - what's the expression? To smile and smile and be a villain? That, I felt, fitted Chen nicely - especially when I found myself looking into his small, dark, unsmiling eyes. The eyes, not of a clerk, but of a man greedy enough to shoot a comrade in cold blood in order to get his reward. Ugh! We should see.

With the help of a Chinese from Special Branch, the Gurkha officer and I questioned Chen minutely about the camp. We wanted to know all we could about it: numbers (anything between twenty and fifty), lay-out, number of *bashas*, approaches and so on. Chen obviously knew what he was talking about, and we drew a rough plan of the camp. He estimated that it would take between two and three days' hard going to reach it, for it lay among the high hills and mountains north-west of Labis, and time was vital. If the operation was to succeed we had to get there before the news of Chen's surrender reached it, or the birds would have flown.

We left at first light, before the rubber tappers were at work, in a downpour of rain. Miserable as this was, it suited us fine. Rain tended to keep the CTs in camp, and it deadened sound. We made good progress in spite of it, with Chen leading and occasionally pointing out signs of CT activity; and when we *'basha-ed'* up for the night, I had a pleasant surprise. The platoon commander produced a flask of rum, a luxury which was issued to all British Army units on ops, but not to the police!

As we sat crouched in our *basha* with the rain belting down, and under the influence of the rum, I quizzed Chen in Malay as to why he'd decided to defect. One reason, he said, was because he didn't see eye to eye with the other Politburo members on the conduct of the war; another, connected with it, was the effect of the SF's measures to cut off their food supplies by the establishment of the 'new villages', like Cha'ah. This policy was really beginning to bite, and finding enough to eat was becoming their main preoccupation. Good news for us. But I also tried to fathom what followed on his defection. Giving himself up, for whatever reason, I could understand; but then to turn on his old pals - that had me beat; and Chen could not, or would not, understand why, in our eyes, such conduct was regarded as despicable.. If it hadn't been for the rum, I might have had second thoughts about sleeping alongside him in our *basha*!

Next day we were away early and made good progress. The rain continued intermittently and in mid-afternoon we came across fresh CT tracks - we knew they were fresh for the rain would have obliterated them otherwise. The problem was that they led off in the wrong direction. The Gurkha officer, Chen and I followed the tracks for a bit and decided they'd probably been made by two couriers. Chen and I agreed that the only thing to do was to ignore them and stick to our plan of getting to the HQ of the NJP as fast as possible. The platoon commander disagreed: he thought they might lead us to a courier camp, perhaps quite close, and we could eliminate that and then continue the main operation. So, since he was in command - and much to Chen's disgust - we set off to follow the trail with one of the Gurkhas acting as leading scout.

This was fine, except that we'd been going for only an hour or so when the heavens opened, the rain fell in buckets, and every trace of footprints was washed clean away. The trail had gone cold. By the time we'd thrashed frantically about in a vain search for further clues, it was getting dark, and there was nothing for it but to camp for the night.

It was then that the platoon commander realised that he was

unable to pinpoint our position. We'd been moving through rugged, hilly country, twisting and turning as we followed the CTs' tracks, having started from what was no more than an unmarked spot in the jungle. Normally this wouldn't have bothered me, but in this case it was vital to pinpoint both our present position and that from which we had deviated. We both studied the map, but to no avail: trying to find one needle in a haystack's bad enough; to try and find two is impossible.

A very dejected party set out next morning in an attempt to retrace our steps. No one was more dejected than Chen, who saw his hopes of a rich reward being washed away in the everlasting rain. For two days after that we continued to search for a fresh starting-point to continue out trek to the NJP headquarters, but it was hopeless. By then our food was finished, and there was no alternative but to slog back to Segamat. I said goodbye to a very downcast Gurkha officer and got a lift back to Cha'ah. I couldn't blame the chap, though I thought he'd made the wrong decision.

A couple of days later I was summoned back to Segamat to face an official enquiry by the District War Executive Committee. When I got there, the Operations Officer, Jock Stirling, raised his eyes to the ceiling.

'What's up?' I asked him.

'SB are hopping made over the NJP fiasco,' he said, 'and they're pinning the blame on you.'

'Well, I'll be damned,' I said. 'Sounds as if Chen's been spinning them a yarn. I'll soon put that right.'

December 1953. Sgt. Shaffie and I. Taken at Cha'ah North Johore, where the 10th Jungle company were based.

Fort Brooke.

A police patrol leaving the Fort for an operation against the CT's.

Aborigines waiting outside my quarters to be paid and given rations. They were hired by me to do many jobs around the fort.

A Temiar tribesman showing off his skills with a blowpipe.

'Home Sweet Home'.
This is the sort of *basha* we would make in the jungle when staying at the same place for several days.

15th June 1954 - captured terrorist Ng Aik Peng. He was so badly hurt during our confrontation that he could not walk. We had to make an improvised stretcher to carry him back to our camp.

Laying out coloured cloth identification marks for an airdrop. A smoke bomb would be ignited and seeing the smoke curling up from the jungle the pilot would home in on it, see the marker and make the drop.

East Johore. Making rafts to cross the Sungei / River Ambat.

My Platoon. Sergeant Shaffie is on my left

And I did, in no mean fashion. I had had no authority whatsoever, I told them; it was a Gurkha operation, and I was simply there as a liaison officer between Chen and the platoon commander. The Gurkha CO backed me up, and that was that. Before I left, however, I suggested to the Committee that I be allowed to borrow Chen and have a crack at the job with my own platoon. The Committee had a think about this, and agreed, and Special Branch handed Chen over to me.

'Take good care of him.' they said.

'I will,' I said.

I set off with my platoon, and Chen, at first light next morning. Nine days had elapsed since his surrender, so time was running out, and we moved fast until we came to the hill country. There the hills are packed as tight as house-roofs, and the going is slow and hard. Normally we would call it a day about four pm, but this was not normal, and I pushed on until the men could go no further.

That evening Shaffie came to me with some disturbing news. I well knew that the men had no time for SEPs like Chen; after all, why should they risk their necks to help the SEPs get rewards greater than anything *they* were ever likely to come by? Now, it seemed, two of my chaps, Talib and Harun, who had had close relatives killed by the CTs, were planning to take their revenge on Chen. If and when we attacked the NJP camp, he would be 'accidentally' caught in the crossfire. That was why he was adamant about having a European officer with him. I remembered the Special Branch injunction to take good care of him and immediately tackled Harun, who was an old hand - and a hard case - about the rumour, and he was all innocence. Harm Chen? The idea had never entered his head; but he knew I didn't believe him, and he was right. Talib, the youngest member of the platoon and a leading scout, was equally emphatic. At least they knew I knew what was up. I didn't mention it to Chen, however.

Next day it was the same hard slog: hills, valleys and more hills. Even Pengerang swamp wasn't as bad as this - but, of course, when I was actually in the swamps I thought longingly of the hills! Instead of rain, we now had sun beating down on us, and I longed for rain. I found myself starting to shiver. Was I going down with fever? Was it the height? No. I realised I was scared stiff, an attack of pre-battle nerves.

We clambered and heaved our way up yet another steep incline and came out on a high ridge, and Chen warned us we were getting close. There would be a sentry stationed on the ridge. Shaffie and I studied the plan of the camp. If we could take out the sentry, we should be able to surprise the camp. According to Chen, the *bashas* were widely separated, and to try and go for all of them would be like trying to catch chickens in a hen-run: we should end up with none. We knew which *basha* was used by the VIPs and we would concentrate on that. One section would tackle the sentry while the other two would be placed as stops to catch anyone trying to escape. The first task was to deal with the sentry.

In fact, the first thing was to deal with Chen, who had developed a hacking cough - ideal for alerting any sentry, even one asleep at his post! In a way, his cough provided a good excuse to keep him out of harm's way during the attack, and I left him to guard our rucksacks. The possibility of the revenge killing had been on my mind, and this resolved the problem very neatly.

Everything was set, and Shaffie and I set off ahead of No.1 Section to identify the sentry-post. One of us led while the other followed, keeping him covered, then the other led, doing the same. Soon we picked up footprints, not many, one here, one there. Chen had told us they were extremely strict about not leaving well-worn tracks to the camp. Carefully, silently, we followed them, first one leading, then the other. We knew that the sentry was armed with a tommy-gun, a fact Chen had passed on with that chilling smile of his. It didn't add to our peace of mind.

It was my turn to lead. The jungle on the ridge was as thick as a hedge; there was no track, no trail, just a random pattern of footprints weaving through the dense tangle of undergrowth. In a yard or two the man ahead vanished as if into thin air.

I stopped, crouched in the shelter of leaves, waiting for Shaffie to join me and take over the lead. It was deathly still, a cloak of silence lying heavy over the jungle, muffling its whispering, broken only by the sudden, blood-curdling screech of some creature, monkey or parakeet, high up in the trees. In this dense and menacing place I crouched and waited. There was no sign of Shaffie. I was alone, and without warning I felt panic rising in my throat, in my mind. I was on a precipice of fear. I felt as if a hundred pairs of eyes were silently watching me through the screen of foliage. I had an insane urge to break and run, run anywhere, get away. It was worse, far worse, than the hunters. A sound to my left. I froze. It was moving towards me. It couldn't be Shaffie - wrong direction. I had to raise my carbine, cock it, be ready to fire. I couldn't move. I was frozen. A figure, glimpsed through the undergrowth. Do something! But I couldn't; I was the rabbit paralysed by the snake. It was getting closer. A whisper. '*Tuan*!' Shaffie. Idiot that I am! Panic ebbed away. He'd lost me; his bren had got snagged in the undergrowth. Nothing unusual; no cause for alarm.

After a breather he took over the lead and I followed. After a few yards, he stopped and pointed. I wormed my way towards him and looked where he was pointing: a small inverted 'V' of dead atap leaves, the mark, as Chen had said, of the sentry-post, only a few yards ahead of us. We waited and listened. No sound. Shaffie edged closer. I covered him with my carbine. Without warning he sprang up and hurled himself towards the sentry-post.

'Shaffie!' I bellowed.

'*Kosang! Kosang!*' he shouted back: 'Empty! Empty!'

We were too late after all. The birds had flown. We had missed them, we reckoned, by a bare twenty four hours. One unfortunate decision and a deluge of rain, and that was that.

# eight

# of ants and elephants

The platoon spent a whole week in the dry and comfortable barracks but we were not idle, for three new men had joined and we spent some time on the firing range. There were other details to be attended to, small things, but important for health and comfort on patrol. One example concerned the rubberised poncho, about seven feet by six feet, with eyelets and press studs all round the edge, with which we were all issued. We always threaded nylon parachute chord through the eyelets before departing on a patrol, so that the poncho could be erected into a *basha* within minutes; and the neck opening was sewn up, for they were never worn as intended. In that hot and humid climate one simply became soaked in sweat, and just as wet as one would have been without it.

At the end of the week, I was briefed for the next operation, which was to find and destroy CT vegetable gardens which had been spotted by Auster observation aircraft in the vicinity of Kambau. Kambau had been an isolated jungle community, but all the inhabitants had been resettled several years before to new villages many miles away, and the jungle in the region had remained unmolested by the Security Forces ever since. When it was a thriving village, the CTs were able to obtain an unlimited supply of food and stores from the inhabitants without risk of interference by the Security Forces. The question was, were they now using it themselves? Kambau lies deep in jungle east of the Kota Tinggi-Mersing road, and our operation was to last a month or more. We would start off with five to six days' rations, and after that we were to be supplied by airdrop.

Before departing on a long operation, I used to have my hair close cropped; it helped to keep ticks, lice and other unwelcome visitors off your head. That done, I would carefully pack my rucksack and always carry Malayan rations rather than the British issue pack. I'd give Jo-Jo a few dollars, and he would purchase dried squid, fish and other eastern delicacies to make life easier in the jungle. It was much simpler than making him cook European meals for me alone. When my rucksack was filled, it weighed over forty pounds. On top of that were the items attached to my belt: a full water-bottle, a thirty six type hand-grenade, *parang*, and toggle rope. Also round my waist would be a bandolier of carbine ammunition; and slung round my neck, map case and compass. All told, I would be carrying fifty pounds or more; but everything was essential, and might mean the difference between life and death if I were lost, or became isolated from the platoon.

There are many theories on how to survive in such circumstances, but my advice to the platoon was not to wander around aimlessly, but, at first light, walk towards the sun for three or four hours, and repeat this every day. By doing this, sooner or later, you would surely get out of the jungle. But can you survive in the jungle like this, without rations or water? Yes, given certain conditions - first and foremost, a determination to survive and the willpower not to give up easily. If you are able to make a shelter and light a fire, you will survive longer. However, there would still be the problem of food; snaring small animals is made to look easy in jungle fiction, but it is anything but simple in reality. Edible fungi and certain roots and fruit can be found, but you have to search for them. There are fish in abundance in the larger streams and rivers, and we all carried hooks and line. Fish traps can be made from rottan which is there for the cutting, providing you have the necessary skill. Water is rarely a problem; if there are no streams you can cut down six foot lengths of the thick, rope-like creepers, and if these are held vertically a light brown watery liquid slowly seeps out. I have actually had to resort to this on three or four occasions, and I can testify that 'water rope' does actually work. In short, someone who is jungle-wise should be able to survive and make his way out of the jungle, but an inexperienced person would have little chance.

While collecting the operations maps for the Kambau region, I was handed the new map reference code which was 'Whisky Soda'. I wrote this on the clear perspex inner cover of my map case, where, when the time arrived, I would juggle with the appropriate numbers and letters to make a six figure MR. Armoured vehicles took us to a point well to the north of Kota Tinggi and as soon as we walked off the road we entered a different world, enveloped once again by the green twilight of the jungle. My pack straps quickly began to cut into my shoulders and my body strained against the weight, especially when I had to crawl and crouch my way underneath fallen trees. My heart went out to the wireless operators, who, between the pair of them, had to carry the radio as well as all their rations and kit.

Our general direction was due east heading for the Sungei

Ambat. I wanted to reach this river by late afternoon but progress proved extremely slow, hampered by the swampy ground which had been made worse by days of heavy rain. Sometimes we were up to our chests in swamp water, and when I halted for rests we had to squat down in the fetid muddy water or loll against a tree. How I wished I could be free of my rucksack instead of having to sit with it clamped to me; it was like a permanent fixture, part of my anatomy.

As we wallowed onwards we noticed that the water was no longer stagnant but was flowing gently southwards, and that the vegetation was no longer that of swamps. I realised we were waist-deep in flooded jungle and, having had this experience a couple of times previously, I knew some of the dangers that lay ahead. The unseen thorn vegetation could snare you and, with your rucksack hampering your release, could easily result in drowning. I altered course and headed northwards, struggling against the current, hoping to get away from it before darkness fell. We had waded only a few hundred yards when luckily we came across a small mound, a tiny island just about big enough for us all to camp on. Free at last from the burden of my rucksack, I felt like Sinbad the Sailor shaking off the Old Man of the Sea from his shoulders. Despite the cramped conditions, Jo-Jo was soon brewing up and producing food. I spoke a few words to the new men, who were absolutely shattered by this introduction to the jungle. It had sapped their energy, but not, fortunately, their spirit.

There was still some daylight, so I left most of the men on the island and took a small patrol further northwards to see if we could get clear of the flood. For two hundred yards or more, the water was still deep, and in a few places our feet were off the ground; if we'd had rucksacks on, we should not have got far. It was a harrowing sensation to be up to your chest in water and at the same time held fast by the thick, thorny and submerged undergrowth. The jungle looked totally different and strange, with trees of all sizes standing upright on this colossal clear table, with all the undergrowth drowned and out of sight. Someone shrieked and a snake went gliding on the water nearby. It scared the hell out of me and I splashed around in a panic. As we pressed on, the water grew shallower, and it was not long before it was only ankle-deep; then we were on dry ground. I made sure we were not on another island, and then altered course to an easterly bearing which would take us to the river. We had covered about five hundred yards when we noticed a highway of sunlight in the jungle ahead of us, breaking through into the trench between the trees created by the river. When we reached it we found it swollen by the rains, but it would quickly revert to normal; and I pointed out to the new men that rivers on maps are not to scale.

We lost no time in returning to the men on the island, and guided the whole platoon to the banks of the river. This was the Sungei Ambat, and here we put up our *bashas*, washed, had a meal and generally sorted ourselves out. I was not at all sure of our exact position, only that we were somewhere along Sungei Ambat. This didn't worry me particularly though, as long as we were able to cross it.

HQ would have to be kept happy, so I started to draft out on a signal pad our estimated MR, using the code 'Whisky Soda'. It was then and only then that my mind clicked. No, it just can't be, I thought; but yes, the clowns have done it again. How could anyone give an MR in code when there were two letters the same? The letter 'S' appeared twice. As I sat pondering over this and deciding what action, if any, to take, the wireless operator handed me a radio message which told me to ignore the MR code. Apparently, one of the other platoon commanders had sent a real sizzler of a message to HQ, blasting the originator for his incompetence. I could not resist the temptation to send out the following message:

'Suggest you change your tincture to "Rum and Coke", which does have ten different letters.'

I did not expect a reply, and I didn't receive one.

Shaffie and I viewed the wide river with some apprehension, and we decided to look for a narrower crossing point.

'Do you think we'll have rain tonight Shaffie?' I asked.

'Don't worry, *Tuan*, the gods will be good to us tonight,' he said reassuringly. I hoped he was right. And he was.

There was no rain that night, and in the morning it was noticeable that the level had fallen, though, it was still a roaring torrent. We trekked along the bank for about a mile, looking for a suitable place to cross. The leading scout pointed out what appeared to be a huge boulder on the water's edge. When we clambered down to inspect it, we found it was a dead elephant, and there were bones of all shapes and sizes littered around at the water's edge - but no sign of the tusks. As a boy I had read of elephant graveyards existing in the deep jungle and here was one; it was like discovering that Father Christmas actually existed.

A few yards from the bones there was a suitable place to cross, but I decided first to search for the tusks.

'*Tuan,* this *gajah* (elephant) is old and has been dead a long time.' Talib said.

'What about the tusks?' I asked'

If we find them,' Talib said, '*banya besar,* (very big) *Tuan*'.

In case there were crocodiles, I tossed two hand-grenades into the river; this, incidentally, produced a supply of fresh fish, as well as scaring off any lurking underwater reptiles. I also set sentries before organising the crossing. Sungei Ambat was still thirty or forty yards across here, and running hard. We joined all our toggle ropes together, and two men swam across taking one end of the rope with them, and fastened it on the other side. Once the line was secured on both sides of the river, a raft was constructed to carry the bren-guns and radio. While this was being done, several of us began diving into the water in the hope of finding the tusks. An assortment of bones were brought to the surface and we piled these together by the skull, but no tusks. Then I felt this long, curved, tusk-shaped object. I grabbed it and shot to the surface with my prize.

'Shaffie, I've got one!' I yelled.

Shaffie came over, examined my treasure, and grinned.

'No, *Tuan*, it's only another bone.'

He was right, and as I sat by the water's edge, listening to it lapping amongst the bones, it was as if the river itself were gently mocking us. Was it also going to oppose our crossing?

The small raft was now completed, and we could ferry the bren-guns and radio across. To give the raft extra buoyancy, we each tied our empty water-bottle to it, but I was ill at ease until it had completed its crossing four times, and its valuable cargo had been safely landed.

Then it was the turn of the platoon. First of all each man placed his poncho flat on the ground and filled it loosely with all his kit, including his weapon. Finally his rucksack, with small branches attached to it, was placed on top of the poncho and the four corners were tied together at the top. He now had a waterproof buoyant vessel which not only contained all his kit, but also provided him with a lifebelt.

It worked a treat, and we propelled ourselves across the river by leg power, without mishap, and without losing a thing. I once told an army officer about my method of river-crossing and he said sceptically, 'But what about the neckhole in the poncho?'

'On my orders, all the platoon have the neck openings sewn up,' I said.

'And when it rains.....?'

'Oh, we carry umbrellas,' I said; and for a second or two, I think he believed me.

Once over the river, we pressed on eastward. The mood of the jungle here was quiet, almost sinister; we heard and saw nothing. After a time we came across elephant tracks. As they were also heading east, I decided to follow them, for it would make the going easier for us. Their track looked as if it had been made by a bulldozer: on either side, saplings had been trampled down and snapped off. Their huge fresh droppings suggested that they were not far in front of us.

By the different sizes of footprints, it looked as if there were several young ones among the herd. For several hundred yards we followed in the wake of the elephants, then we heard sounds of tearing foliage and the snapping of branches. It grew louder, and, rounding a bend in the track, we saw the herd in a small clearing. I had to try and get a photograph, and cautiously began to move closer to them. Shaffie whispered in alarm, '*Tuan jaga baik.* (Sir, be very careful.) They have young. They're dangerous. Take care.'

'I will,' I said. But I badly wanted some pictures, and so, very cautiously, I crept towards them with my camera at the ready. When I was within about twenty yards of them, I began to click away. There were about ten of them, the adults lazily tearing and ripping away at the foliage, the young ones capering round close to their parents. It was fantastic to see them like this, in the wild, and I started to steal nearer for a close-up. One of the adults slowly hinged his ears round; then a second threw back his massive head, his trunk in the air. They all started to drum the ground with their feet, and then the trumpeting began. As it reached a crescendo, the adults, with trunks held high, charged towards me. I held my ground, still clicking away. Shaffie was yelling, urging me to run; and run I did, as they came thundering down on me with a sound of splintering trees and tearing undergrowth. The air was filled with a drumming roar which vibrated the earth. My pack hindered me, and I slithered and almost fell. They were not great lumbering beasts any more, but extraordinarily fleet of foot, and they were gaining on me. I was really scared now. I jettisoned my pack, and, free of its encumbrance, ran for my life. Anything to escape from that deafening stentorian trumpeting and screeching, those earth-shaking feet.

As I ran, I unhooked the hand-grenade from my belt, ready, as a last resort, to toss it amongst them. I shouted to the men to drop their packs and run too, and the jungle became littered with rucksacks as we made good our escape. Gradually the bellowing, trumpeting and huffing died away; they had gone blundering off in another direction. We waited a little to make sure, then crept back to retrieve our packs. Next to my rucksack was a giant footprint; luckily they had just missed it. It had been a near thing all the same. Next time, I would certainly *jag baik*!

When we later halted for a bite, Shaffie and I laughed, somewhat ruefully, over the incident, and PC Tahir said he was disappointed that I'd failed to collect some elephants' tear drops. According to the Malays, these tears are priceless: a few drops sprinkled on the girl a man wishes to marry, and she cannot refuse him. How one actually obtains tear drops from a crying elephant still has me puzzled. PC Tahir was the platoon's ladies' man. He was a big, lumbering, warm-hearted fellow, and liked nothing better than to gather an audience round his *basha* in the evenings and regale them with stories of his innumerable conquests. I don't think anyone believed them, but they relieved the tedium of jungle camps. Of course, he may have been telling the truth.

On one occasion, during a kit inspection, I came across a number of curious objects among his gear. They were small furry or hairy rings, an inch or so in diameter. I asked him what they were for, whereupon he blustered and became extremely embarrassed, and the other men who were present started sniggering.

'Come on, Tahir' I said. 'Tell me. What are they?'

Poor Tahir hung his head and mumbled something about them being goat's eyelashes, and I suddenly twigged.

'Well, Tahir,' I said, 'I never thought that you, of all men, would need such artificial stimuli'.

'No, no *Tuan*,' he muttered. 'Not me. It's the women. They love them.'

So that was the secret of his conquests! But he was a sterling character, one of my best bren-gunners, the sort of chap I was glad to have around.

They have other odd customs connected with courtship. Some Malayan women, in order to get their man, lift up their sarongs and straddle a bowl of very hot and steaming rice (in Malay, *Nasi*) for several minutes. They then serve this rice - which is known as '*Nasi* Stand at Ease' - to the man of their choice. This is why, on a number of occasions in the *kampongs*, the men refused to have their rice cooked by the villagers. More than once, when Jo-Jo had arranged with some kind family to cook my food and I was just settling down to enjoy my curry and rice, one of the platoon comedians would sidle up to me and mutter '*Nasi* Stand at Ease, *Tuan*' and, at the same time, point out some wizened old village woman. '*Nasi* Stand at Ease!'

That evening saw us in a comfortable base camp, but I could not fix our position; all I knew was that we were somewhere between the Sungei Ambat and the east coast. I desperately wanted to know our exact position, and the only way I could find out was to climb a nearby tree and take bearings on any natural features that I could see. There was no question of scaling the really huge trees with their great buttresses, standing there like moon rockets ready for blast-off, for all their branches are near the top.

Others though were possible. I selected one and, taking my hand-bearing compass with me, heaved myself up amongst the sturdy branches. Higher and higher I climbed, until, like a diver surfacing, I broke through the canopy of foliage and into the bright sunlight, away from the submarine gloom below. Thus, fumbling with my compass and precariously holding on to a slender branch, I managed to take bearings on several high features in the distance, which I should have been able to identify on the map. Suddenly, I felt myself being viciously stung on the back of my neck. Instinctively I slapped and scratched the spot; my hand was covered with ants. And now they were all over my body; my uniform was black with them and so were all the branches. They were on my head, my face, inside my shirt and trousers. I must have wrecked an ants' nest on my way up; they were thick on every branch, out in force in their millions, their legions advancing towards me. There was no escape from them.

The boughs higher up were not strong enough to support even my mere nine stone, and in any event they would have taken over the upper reaches of the tree in a matter of minutes. I could not afford to sit it out, like some bird at the top, waiting for them to go away. I had to escape, and the only way was down; but the whole tree trunk was alive with them. My body was smarting, and I had to snort down my nostrils to keep them out; they were all over my face and in my ears. I had to let go with one hand to poke them out. As I climbed down, with my body pressed against the trunk, the brutes came with me. With both arms locked around the trunk I was at their mercy, and they made the most of it as they scampered and raced unchecked all over me. I clamped my mouth shut, but they stung my lips; I closed my eyes tight, and they stung my eyelids; I shook my head vigorously, hoping to dislodge them, but it made no difference. Half crazy with their stinging, I half-slid, half-fell down the tree, and landed with a jolt at the bottom. Thank God the river was close by. I threw myself in, clothes and all, and stayed there until all the last of them had drowned or swum ashore.

'We call them *api ant, Tuan,*' "Fire Ant",' Shaffie said.

'Not a bad name for them'.

'But there are usually no ill effects from their bites,' he said.

'That's something,' I said. I was stinging and itching all over, and my lips and eyelids were swollen.

'And I'll tell you another good thing,' I said, 'where there's ants there's no lice.'

'I think I'd rather have lice,' he said laughing.

When he and I worked out our position from the bearings I had taken, we found it was well to the north of my original estimate. So that evening I was able to give HQ the correct MR of our camp, and the MR for our forthcoming airdrop, which would be Kambau itself. That evening Shaffie and I talked far into the night, mainly about our various encounters - some humorous, others not at all - with mammals, reptiles, bats, insects, and a host of other creatures. In my *basha* that night, I thought of my two escapades that day: were they humorous? Elephants and ants were about as far apart as possible in size, yet each could create havoc in its particular way. An encounter with either tended to be funnier afterwards than it was at the time.

From 'Ant Camp' we headed south-east for Kambau, where I hoped to arrive by early afternoon. For the first few hours we were still in thick primary jungle, and there were no signs of CTs; but as this gave way to secondary jungle I knew we were not far from our goal. Secondary jungle, where the trees have been cut down and secondary growth of every kind - bushes, trees, creepers and bamboo - has taken over, is more difficult to move through, depending on the time which has elapsed since the clearing operation took place. Five or six years had passed since the inhabitants of Kambau were moved, and the area had once again returned to nature. Our progress was slow for we literally had to hack our way through the dense scrub and undergrowth. Occasionally we came across areas of *lalang*, the six foot high grass in which you are exposed to the sun, and also get a hot haze off the ground. Usually it pays to skirt around it; but in this case there were so many pockets of it in the region that we carved our way through.

At last we came across collapsed and decayed buildings, and knew we had arrived in Kambau. None was habitable; roofs had caved in, creepers had snaked through doorways and windows. I hacked my way into the remains of one house, to find the bric-a-brac left by its former owners - a broken mirror, bits of crockery, rusted cooking utensils. But none of the buildings we searched showed any sign of CT activity.

I decided to make our base camp by a small, collapsed bridge on the edge of the *kampong*; we needed a good site as we would be there for about five days; in fact, whenever we were to stay out for a couple of nights or more, we always made ourselves as comfortable as possible. Then *bashas* take on a more permanent appearance: some of the men make small platforms for their belongings; water points on the river's edge are established; undergrowth is cleared from inside the camp perimeter to give freedom of movement. Although we scavenged round the ghost village, it produced nothing of value, though we came across the local Chinese temple and burial ground, a bit too close to our camp for comfort.

That evening Shaffie and I discussed the areas of cultivation which were roughly north-east from our position, and it was decided that we would each check out a section. I favoured the one by the side of a river, but trying to find a small allotment in the jungle can prove extremely difficult. The most effective method is that known as 'aiming off' : instead of following the bearing that would, if you were lucky, take you straight to the objective, you 'aim off' on a bearing well to one side of it. In this instance, I planned to 'aim off' to the south, then when I reached the river, I could follow it northwards until I came to it. I'd once had the frustrating experience of steering a direct course for an objective, not finding it, and then having to search in both directions instead of only one.

We set off the next morning, and as we were travelling light and the sun was not yet at full blast we were able to negotiate the secondary jungle without much difficulty, but we were still pleased when we finally found ourselves in proper jungle. We found no sign of CTs, though there were plenty of animal tracks, including more elephants' trails going in our direction but we kept well clear of them.

Because of 'aiming off', when we reached the river I was sure that the allotment we were looking for must be only four hundred yards or so northwards. Stealthily now, we followed the twisting river, and after about three hundred yards saw the sunlight streaming into a clearing. We crept forward to the edge, but saw and heard nothing. Then we realised that it wasn't an allotment at all, but simply a natural clearing. From the air it might have looked like a vegetable garden, especially as the pilot would not have dared to investigate for fear of warning the CTs that they had been spotted. We continued to scout the area until mid-afternoon, but found nothing and returned to camp. Shaffie was already there; he had drawn a blank also. During the following days we visited the other suspected clearings but they were the same; not a hint nor a whiff of CT evidence did we come across.

Next day we were due for our airdrop, so everyone stayed in base, though in this case, as there were open clearings near at hand for the DZ, no lumberjacking was necessary. All that was required was to lay out the bright fluorescent orange nylon markers in the *lalang* adjoining our base camp; then, when I heard the aircraft, I would explode a phosphorus bomb, the smoke of which would help the crew to spot us. A few minutes later the aircraft was thundering overhead. I chatted to the pilot over the radio. It was only when he wished me a 'Happy Christmas' that it dawned on me that Christmas Day could not be far off. I knew we'd started the operation on the 19th December but I soon lose track of days and dates when on operations. I can always ask the radio operators, which I did this time; it was the 23rd December. When we checked the stores after the drop, we were delighted to find a crate containing ten live hens for our Christmas dinner, but we were a little puzzled to find in another crate two five-gallon drums of black paint! As I could think of no conceivable use for black paint in our particular circumstances, I punctured the cans with my *parang* and let the black liquid seep away into the ground. We kept the chickens until Christmas day, and I must admit it was an unusual sight to see a tethered chicken pecking and scratching outside every *basha*.

On Christmas Day itself, I sent no patrols out, the chickens were put down in the traditional Moslem way, and Jo-Jo made full use of his culinary skills to provide a real jungle banquet. It was far from being a typical English Christmas dinner, but I gave Jo-Jo full marks for what he produced over a small wood fire with limited utensils - even though I declined his offer of fried lizard for a starter. And, of course, I was the only one in the platoon to appreciate Christmas - they were all Moslems - so I had no one to share it with. On Boxing Day we pulled out of the deserted village of Kambau to try our luck to the south-east.

Several airdrops and many weary miles of trekking and swamp-wallowing later, we made our way thankfully out of that damp and deadly environment. For over a month we had trawled through the vast jungle area of Kambau without finding the slightest evidence of CT movement. After that, I was hardly surprised to find that none of my photographs had come out; the shopkeeper suggested that somehow water seemed to have got into the camera. I was sorry not to have my first-hand shots of a charging bull elephant, all the same.

among the aboriginies: the trouble with pangoi

In October 1954 I was appointed commander of Fort Brooke[6], one of a chain of small permanent camps that had been established during the previous two years along the four hundred mile spine of Malaya as part of the 'Briggs Plan'. Before I walked in with a section from the Cameron Highlands, I spent a few days at the police headquarters in Kuala Lumpur, being briefed on what was obviously going to be a difficult and daunting task. Nor should I have my invaluable Shaffie: we had said goodbye at Cha'ah, and he had given me a Malayan kris as a parting gift.

In common with the other fort, Brooke was in an area inhabited by aborigines, in this case the Temiar Senoi, who were believed to be under CT influence. It was tucked away in deep mountainous jungle on the Perak-Kelantan border, 2,300 feet above sea level, and was one of the seven forts in that outlandish 10,000 square miles south of the Thai frontier. It would be difficult to imagine a place more utterly remote. My platoon and I would be entirely on our own, our only contact with the outside world being the radio, the arrival of the occasional helicopter with some bunch of VIPs and the supplies regularly parachuted in to us by the RAF.

At police HQ I was given an outline of the job I had to do. The main purpose of all the forts was to win over the aborigines, who were, or might be, subject to pressure from the Communists, and whose loyalty was in the balance. Among the various inducements on offer were, first and foremost, medical supplies; but also food, paid work, and simple tools. Major E.C.V. Peacock of the Royal Engineers, who was responsible for setting up Fort Brooke, mentioned in a letter to me the particular value of six inch nails: three of them could be fashioned by the Temiar into a trident for fishing:

> My popularity in rewarding aborigines with three six inch
> nails....for information or good work, was worth all the untruths
> (needed to obtain them from Police Supplies). With fourteen
> nails to the pound I considered it a cheap form of goodwill.

The headman at Fort Brooke was Mentri Awol, and it was vital that I kept on good terms with him.. But I also had to try and win over - or eliminate - a basically hostile aborigine named Pangoi, who was reputed to have around ninety followers. I also had to kill or capture the CT Ah Ming, who was in league with Pangoi. Ah Ming was the local administrator of the twenty strong Communist organisation, ASAL, which aimed to control the aborigines in deep jungle. Ah Ming and his gang used to visit the various *ladangs* (clearings) in small groups, looking for food and information, and then slip away to their main camp. In addition, I was expected to undertake regular patrols and gather as much information as possible on the CTs in the area.

The assignment sounded both intriguing and challenging. Before I left Kuala Lumpur, the Major in the Intelligence Branch who had been briefing me promised to come and assess the situation for himself, though pressure of work in the office, he said, meant that it would not be for some weeks. Somehow 'pressure of work' never eased enough for him to make it - but this did not entirely surprise me.

Helicopters were only for the privileged few. I walked from the Cameron Highlands, where I was met by a section from the fort. It took two days and a night, if you were fit - as I was - and had a good guide and so I didn't have to bother with map and compass. At last, we broke out of the forest into a wide clearing beside the river, the Sungei Brok. On a mound were half a dozen *atap*-roofed *bashas* arranged in a rough triangle, the whole thing enclosed within a perimeter fence of barbed wire. On the level ground, beyond the fence, was the *ladang* of Mentri Awol with its little collection of longhouses. There were two entrances, one in the north-west, the other in the south-east, where a long flight of steps led down, past the name FORT BROOKE in large white letters, to the helicopter landing-ground and dropping-zone.

The camp itself was quite small, each side of the triangle being no more than two hundred yards long. The three *bashas* along the south-east side contained my quarters and a spare room for guests; the ops, radio and a barrack room, and stores. To the north were another barrack room and the guardroom and office, with the cookhouse and a couple of other buildings on the remaining side. There were a few spindly trees in the compound, in the centre of which was a bunker which I called 'The Alamo'. Just outside the triangle, and on two sides of it, were gun-pits big enough for two or three men. On the remaining side, the land fell steeply eighty feet to the river. Bamboo grew thickly there, and it had been interlaced with barbed wire to form, with the sheer drop, a natural defence. At each corner of the triangle was a bren-gun post, and these were manned all the time, with stand-to at dawn and dusk. There was also a plan, 'Operation Medal', for recapturing the fort in the event of it ever falling into CT hands.

When I had dumped my kit and settled in, I had a good look around. So this was to be my home and workplace for the next six months. I felt a certain thrill, not unmixed with anxiety, as I took it all in. Would I, I wondered, be able to make friends with Mentri Awol and his tribesfolk, or sort out Pangoi and his followers, or the devious Ah Ming? Well, we should see.

I had my first meeting with Mentri Awol soon after my arrival. As I was to see him regularly over the coming months, and as he was my most important contact with the aborigines, I'd better try and describe him. A small, squat body on bow legs, rather stout for an aborigine, with a belly that sagged over his tatty *chowat* or loincloth. But it was his feet that first caught my attention. As a result of having padded through the jungle barefoot all his life, they were huge and flat, with stubby, splayed toes, and hardened like tyre treads. His ankles were scarred by leech-bites which must have gone septic, leaving large blotches of polished skin. When he coughed and spat, which he did continuously, he revealed very few and very black teeth. He didn't know how old he was, but my guess was that he was over fifty.

I would have dealings with him most days, and the procedure was always the same. He would shamble into my room, and at once his eyes - a sort of mud colour, laced with thin crimson threads - would start to roam over my table, searching for some new wonder to examine. To him, a torch or a pair of scissors was the height of technology and always a source of curiosity and delight. He also adored magazines, whether upside down or the right way up - it made no difference. I can see him now, standing there like some jungle goblin, one hand holding his blowpipe, the other scratching his belly, his bloodshot eyes roaming round and always coming to rest when they spotted cigarettes. A grin would split that ugly mug of his, showing those dreadful teeth.

'*Rokok, Tuan*?' He couldn't understand why I didn't smoke. I had no interpreter; we conversed in a mixture of Malay and the few words of his tongue I was able to pick up. However, the aborigines' vocabulary is very limited, so we managed to understand each other somehow. I usually gave him a mug of tea and something to eat, and as he slurped and chewed, he would question me.

'How many rivers and mountains do you have to cross to return to your own people?' or 'What sort of animals roam your land?'

In turn, I would ask him what life in his *ladang* was like before the Japanese came, or the Communists; this would lead to the question of Pangoi and Ah Ming.

As time went on - and I know I'm jumping ahead here - a kind of bond, almost a friendship, was created between us. I must admit I did my best to encourage it. For one thing, it would become known to the others and perhaps persuade them to come over - as indeed it did. For another, he could be a useful source of information; moreover, if he was on my side, my own safety would be that much greater. In fact, later on, this bond was to save my life. When I left the fort at the end of my tour, he gave me his blowpipe, which I still have.

It took me some weeks to sort out who was who; but eventually I discovered that one of the aborigines to be seen about the camp was the son of the CT-inclined Pangoi, and that he was in regular touch with his father. I gave this lad, Alok, some cigarettes, and asked him to present them to his father with my compliments, in the hope that I should learn his father's whereabouts. No such luck, and yet I was determined to try and lure him into the fort and persuade him to surrender.

This may sound naive, but so attractive to the aborigines were the things we had to offer, and so efficient their jungle telegraph, that some of them would travel considerable distances when they learnt that a new fort was being built. However, Pangoi was too wary to fall for that. Although I sent him small parcels of cigarettes, rock salt - for which all the aborigines had a craving - rice and tinned food, he continued to lie low. As I had a shrewd idea that he would hand over some of the stuff to Ah Ming, I kept the gifts small, and always punctured the tins so that the contents would last only a few days.

I soon realised that a great deal of patience was going to be required to achieve anything with these apparently simple people, so I kept my ear to the ground and hoped for a break.

In the meantime, life at the fort went on in its strange, isolated, uneventful way, punctuated by the weekly airdrop of supplies, the occasional arrival of a chopper, and regular patrols in the surrounding country.

Friday was the big day, with the arrival of much-needed stores. Two RAF Valettas would come weaving their way amongst the mountains, fly low over the fort, and launch their parachute-borne loads above the DZ. Usually their aim was excellent, and the boxes and bundles of barbed wire, ammunition, cement, petrol, clothes, medicines and rations (including one meal of fresh bread and meat) would float down on target. Inevitably there were misjudgements; loads would go astray and land in the compound or threaten our frail huts. On one memorable occasion, when a parachute failed to open, five five-gallon tins of petrol landed like a bomb on the cookhouse and went straight through the roof, burst and showered petrol all round. The fire was alight, and it was only the swift action of the cook, who dashed in among the debris and smothered it, that saved the camp from being burnt to the ground. The petrol-soaked *atap* and bamboo would have blown up like a paint factory.

The supply department was pretty good, all things considered; one item I requested was a petrol-engined water-pump, which I happened to know was rusting away, unused, in the stores of No.2 PFF.

'Your pump will be on the next available helicopter' came the reply to my signal.

I was delighted: it would be much more efficient than my team of aborigines, trudging up from the river with their five-gallon drums and bamboo containers.

Sure enough, a few days later a chopper duly turned up. As

soon as I heard the familiar engine-noise I dashed down to the landing-zone to guide it in, and out stepped an immaculately dressed senior police officer, festooned with cameras like an American tourist.

'And my water-pump, Sir?' I asked when I had greeted him.

'Water-pump? No, I know nothing about it'.

While I hadn't expected it to be delivered in person by this dapper gentleman, I had assumed it would be on board. But he was only interested in inspecting the fort and taking snaps of the 'natives'. That evening he would be back in the club, regaling his fellow officers with his experiences and holding forth about the aborigines - a subject on which, of course, he was now an expert.

In the end I never did get the pump. After half a dozen more vain requests I received a signal to say that it was seized up and unserviceable. The water-carriers carried on.

The police officer with the cameras wasn't my only visitor, and most of them were nothing but a damn nuisance. One wanted the slit trenches moved further from the perimeter fence; another - soon afterwards - thought they should be nearer to it. A third said he'd seen a much superior dropping-zone about three-quarters of a mile away, and suggested I should transfer our activities there.

'What about carting the supplies to the fort?' I asked. Oh, that was simple, a narrow-gauge railway could be laid, and small trucks- pulled, presumably, by a miniature steam-engine - would do the job. I learnt to listen to these geezers, agree with everything they said, and see them off, back to their cool, clean offices in Kuala Lumpur, with a sense of relief. When I couldn't get even a simple water-pump, I could imagine the likelihood of obtaining a narrow-gauge railway with locomotive! The geese were another of their brain waves. These two birds were intended to warn us of the approach of CT intruders during the night. They certainly made enough racket, and for the first few nights I had very little sleep as their hissing woke me and had me reaching for the bren; only what they were hissing at was our own sentries. After that I penned them up at night - and they came in very handy at Christmas.

These tiresome, but harmless, diversions did not distract me from my main objective, first to win the loyalty of Mentri Awol and his aborigines, second to run Pangoi and Ah Ming to earth. It was in connection with the second that I came up against the Department of Aborigines at Kuala Lumpur and their Assistant Protector, Mrs Gouldsbury.

Pam Gouldsbury (later MBE) had spent many years in South Africa, but had come to Malaya and married the superintendent of the Field Force, which was in charge of aborigine operations. She then became involved with the aborigines herself. This gave her a greater authority than if she had been simply a member of the department. I got on very well with her, though some of the fort commanders resented the fact that a woman could arrive out of the blue and tell them what they could and could not do. On this one occasion, I must admit that I should have found it easier to deal with a man: I could have told him straight to buzz off. With her I couldn't - what happened was this.

     Weeks had gone by since I had first tried to win over Pangoi and his followers, but I had had no success at all. Then, one day, one of my informers came to tell me that he knew which *ladang* Pangoi was staying in, and that he was prepared to guide me there. I was cock-a-hoop: at last my chance had come, and I jubilantly announced the fact to Pam Gouldsbury, who happened to be on one of her periodic visits to the fort. I was on to a good thing at last, I said; I should be off at first light in the morning to try and capture him or, if he resisted, kill him as I would any other CT sympathiser. To my amazement, she absolutely forbade it.

'But,' I said, 'that's one of the main reasons I'm here. I'm sorry, but this is too good a chance to miss.'

'In that case,' she said, 'you must let me send a signal at once to the department.'

'Very well,' I said, and, like an idiot, I actually sent her message myself.

Back came the reply from aborigine HQ, Kuala Lumpur: 'Nothing doing! No action to be taken against Pangoi.' What was going on? This, after all, was the man who, with Ah Ming and his followers, had ambushed and killed three British soldiers not far from the fort only a few months previously. But argument was hopeless. *Her* job was to protect the aboriginal inhabitants: the fact that he was an acknowledged CT carried no weight with her, for we were doing different jobs.

The episode was all the more tiresome because I liked the woman and respected her for the work she was doing. What's more, she was extremely kind and thoughtful to me. On each of the three occasions that she visited me, she always brought something to make life a bit more tolerable, such as a bottle of whisky or some magazines. Once, when I had been suffering from bad feet (the skin was rotting between and under my toes and dropping off like bits of tripe), she organised a tin of foot powder by the next airdrop. On another occasion, when she found we only had one spoon in the fort, she arranged for half a dozen to be sent in.

Talking of rotting feet, that wasn't the only health problem I had to deal with. Malaria, of course, and another brand of jungle fever, were common and easy to treat with quinine and M & B tablets; but when I discovered that two chaps, who had arrived with the relieving garrison platoon, had VD, that was another matter. I retired to the medical room to consult the book of words. 'Penicillin should be given intravenously,' it said. Hmm! I'd never given an injection in my life, and the fort's medical orderly hadn't either, and was afraid to try. Nor had anyone told me that the best thing to practise on is an orange - not that we had any oranges in Fort Brooke. Anyway, in they trooped at seven pm, as instructed.

'Relax' I said, 'there's nothing to it, no problem.'

I had selected the smallest needle, with the mistaken idea that this would make it easier. In fact, the penicillin was rather viscous, and it took me ages to force it through the narrow gauge needle and into their arms; so much so that I had to take a break halfway through, leaving the needle dangling from the wretched lad's arm while I took a deep breath and tried a different grip. In the end I was using the heel of my hand in order to force it through; then the syringe slipped through my sweaty fingers, and the needle went in up to the hilt. You should have heard him yell! And, of course, the one who was waiting for his jab was horror-struck. In my defence, I have to say that my debut as a medic was taking place by the flickering light of a hurricane lamp.

There was an amusing follow-up to that evening's work. It must have been three years later. I was held up in traffic at a police road-block and a very smart police constable came to the car.

'*Tuan* Follows, Fort Brooke?' he asked me.

'Yes!' I said. 'Were you there?'

He jabbed at his upper arm with his finger.

'You remember, *Tuan*?'

I recognised his face then and laughed. 'No more trouble?'

'No *Tuan*, thank you.'

'Good. You didn't know you were my first patient, did you?'

He looked suitable amazed. 'No, *Tuan*.'

'But it worked, didn't it.'

Jungle policeman? Jungle bleeding doctor!

My ploy to capture Pangoi had been thwarted, and my informant was disgusted with me.

'What's the use of my risking my life to obtain information when you do nothing about it?' he demanded.

'Well,' I said, knowing that the aborigines were deeply superstitious, especially where dreams were concerned, 'I had this dream about Pangoi the very night after you came to me. If I had gone and perhaps killed him, his spirit would have haunted both of us.' I knew I'd hit the mark. After a moment, he replied.

'*Tuan* believes in dreams, then, just like jungle folk do. Good.'

I'd saved the situation, but I hadn't got Pangoi, so I had to think of something else, and my next idea was to try and arrange a parley with him. So I sent for the elders, Mentri Awol, Mentri Kechril and Busu Jamin[7] - whom I did not trust - and we went to Mentri Awol's longhouse to discuss a new plan I'd thought up. Mentri Awol's *ladang* was the one overlooked by the fort; and one of the reasons why I never had any trouble from the CTs while I was there was that I told him right from the start that if I did, I should blow it to smithereens.

Longhouses were all on much the same plan; built of bamboo, roofed with *atap*, and raised three feet or so above the ground. Mentri Awol's typically, was one hundred feet long, and forty of his people lived in it. Forty people, all apparently coughing their guts up and spitting between the slats of the bamboo floor if they had a good enough aim, on to the chickens that lived underneath.

I shall never forget my first impressions as I climbed up the rickety steps and gingerly picked my way across the springy bamboo floor. It was gloomy for a start, and thick with the smoke from the fire which burnt continuously in a sort of earthen grate in the middle. No wonder they never stopped coughing! Each family had a sort of fenced-in pen, about six feet square, in which they lived their domestic lives with little or no regard to the others doing the same thing on either side. Privacy, I decided, must be in the mind!

I spoke to one or two of the womenfolk. Most of them seemed to be no more than thirteen or fourteen, but as aborigines can't count to more than ten (after that, any number is 'plenty') there was no means of telling. Some of them were naked from the waist up. They took no more notice of me than they did of the flies that buzzed around their breasts.

In this twilight smog the three elders and I, together with the other inhabitants who had been drawn into the conference, discussed what to do. I wanted to meet Pangoi and I said as much. At this, there was much head-wagging, and I left them to it and went to the far end of the hut while they made up their minds, drawn by one of the men who was lying groaning in pain. I had a look at him; under a covering of leaves and the remains of a filthy poultice of wood ash, his leg had a large, gaping suppurating gash. I cleaned and dressed the wound as best I could, and told the aborigines to take him into the fort for proper treatment. At first, they wouldn't hear of it, but at last, after a lot of noisy discussion, they agreed to do as 'Dr Follows' said! At the other end of the longhouse, some decision seemed to have been reached, and I rejoined them.

'Would the *Tuan*,' Mentri Awol asked me, 'be prepared to meet Pangoi at a place of his choosing?'

'I'll meet him anywhere he likes,' I said.

And so it was arranged that Alok would act as the emissary. After this, I was invited to 'dinner' - a fish which I'd seen being cooked inside a small length of bamboo in the ashes. Once cooked, it was taken out and put on a large leaf, and everyone helped themselves.

Picture the scene, if you can. The longhouse, lit only by chinks of light filtering through the gaps in the bamboo walls; rancid with smoke and the smell of human bodies, and now, of roasted fish; full of dark shapes, men, women and children, squatting round the fire and digging into the fish with fingers, some of them dry and flaky with *korab*, a disease which, rather like my feet, shed bits of skin into the food. I would have been unforgivably inhospitable to have refused, but I can't say I dug in with much relish. A policeman's lot is not always a happy one, but interesting, you must admit.

A little time before this, I had received information about a CT camp in the neighbourhood, and, what was more, my informant was prepared to guide me to it. This was most unusual; they nearly always made some excuse.

'How many in the camp?' I asked him.

'Few, *Tuan*'

That, in the light of their vagueness over numbers, might be anything from two to ten.

'How far is it?'

'Well, *Tuan*, on the way back I slept three times, rolled and smoked some cigarettes, and caught some fish,' he explained after several minutes of deep thought.

'Did you sleep only at night?'

'Oh, no, *Tuan*, I sleep in the sun too.'

'Do you smoke much?'

'I smoke plenty, *Tuan*.'

'How many a day?'

'Plenty.'

From riddles like this, it was hardly simple to decide where the camp would be, how far, or how many CTs might be there. I decided, wrongly in the event, that it was probably half a days march, and I planned accordingly. I decided to take six chaps with me, and off we went with our guide. After two hours of trekking, I asked him, 'How much further?' to which the inevitable reply came, 'Far, *Tuan*.' I was in no mood for further questioning. Our guide abruptly halted after another half-hour's trekking. Pointing to a barely distinguishable track, he told me this led to the camp, but it was still far he said.

He then refused to act as guide any longer and attached himself to a safe position at the rear of our small patrol instead. So I changed my carbine for the bren-gun, took up position as leading scout and, using the best of my tracking ability, led the section. The track promptly led us into a bamboo thicket, which was almost impossible to penetrate. The canes, which can grow up to six inches in diameter and tower forty feet or more, spring up in all directions from the ground. One minute you are wriggling on your belly under horizontal stems, the next you are trying to squeeze between the bars of a cage. Mixed up with the growing canes are others that have broken off, on which it's all too easy to impale yourself; and bamboo cuts nearly always turn septic.

As my greatest concern at that moment was to escape from that bamboo prison, I forgot about other possible dangers ahead. Suddenly I became aware of a movement to my front; a CT sentry was standing a few yards away and bringing his rifle up into the firing position, pointing straight at me. I was trapped, caught like an animal in a snare by the bamboo. Luckily for me he was off target, and the couple of rounds he fired whistled harmlessly past me. I managed to disentangle the bren and loosed off; but instead of a burst, it fired only once, and that missed. The bloody bamboo had flipped the control lever from automatic to single rounds. As fast as we could, we plunged out of the thicket and assaulted the camp, only to find it empty, except for a couple of packs and a large pool of blood. We couldn't even mount a follow-up as I had to be back in the fort before darkness, and anyway we hadn't brought any food with us.

On of the packs contained, among other things, documents and photographs. A Chinese PC in the patrol examined the documents. The pack belonged to Ah Ming. In one of the other packs was a tin of cured dog flesh. There was nothing else of interest, so we burnt the camp and set off back to the fort. Round one to Ah Ming.

The rendezvous with Pangoi was arranged. We were to meet at a *ladang* some miles from the fort, and I was to go there with a small patrol. What I didn't know was that Ah Ming had got to hear of it and it was he, not Pangoi, who had set it up. I was put in the picture when Mentri Awol came shuffling and spitting into my shack just before we were due to leave.

'What brings you here, Mentri?' I asked.

'You must not go to meet Pangoi.'

'Why ever not?'

'They will kill you.'

'Who will?'

'Ah Ming, *Tuan*.'

Slowly, I got the whole thing out of him. Ah Ming and a handful of the aborigines who were hostile to us, having persuaded me that the arrangement was genuine, were to lay an ambush where our route crossed a wide, shallow river, where we would have no cover. There, the bullets and the silent and deadly *ipoh*-tipped darts from their blowpipes would come whizzing out of the bush before we even knew what was happening. All six of us would have died in agony in the shoal water, without ever having lifted a weapon to defend ourselves.

As I listened to the chilling details of the plot, I couldn't help wondering if Mentri Awol hadn't had a hand in it and then got cold feet. Either way, he'd done me a good turn, and I resigned myself to his coming hawking and spitting into my shack - and leaving his little visitors behind him - even if it meant scratching myself just as he did. I sent off for anti-lice powder, but it was a week before the next drop, and during that week the little buggers seemed to increase ten-fold.

On his next visit, Mentri Awol brought even more disturbing news: Pangoi was willing to discuss surrender terms, but only on condition that I met him alone and unarmed. This was a possibility that had never occurred to me and as soon as I'd agreed I regretted it, even though I had insisted that the meeting took place in Mentri's *ladang* and nowhere else.

'Understand, Mentri,' I said, 'if so much as one shot is heard from the *ladang,* my men will have orders to rake the place with everything they've got.'

The threat might not save me; I wouldn't even give the order, but, if it were a trap, bluff was all the protection I could think of. Mentri swore there was nothing to worry about, but the more I thought about it the less I liked it, and I spent a wretched afternoon, finally going for a swim in the river.

I was no sooner in the cool, turbulent waters of the Sungei Brok than I was summoned back to the fort. This is it, I thought, as

I slowly dried myself, dressed, and trudged up the hill. To my surprise, just inside the compound, was Mentri, and with him another man whom I didn't recognise. Could this be Pangoi? The man had been in my head for so long, yet I had no mental picture of him. As I approached, any doubts were swept away: he gave me the clenched-fist salute of the Communist. I curtly told him to drop it; he did so, and we shook hands. I began to size him up: above average height, good physique, a straggling grey moustache, and extremely shifty eyes. I didn't know what had made him decide to surrender, but my instincts told me, whatever else you do, don't trust him. And my instincts proved to be right,

ten

whose ambush?

To celebrate Pangoi's surrender, I suggested to Mentri Awol that his people put on a *sewang*, the traditional aborigine dance. He agreed on condition that I supplied the grub, which was fair enough. The 'entertainment' was scheduled for eight o'clock that same night in the fort.

By the flickering light of a bonfire, the musicians took their places. Half a dozen girls, armed with pieces of bamboo of varying lengths, squatted on the ground in front of a stout log. Slowly at first, this primitive orchestra started to tap out a rhythm, wood against wood, and the first dancers - all men or all women, never mixed - moved round within the circle of spectators, shuffling and chanting. Round and round they went. The speed of the rhythmic drumming increased. Faster and faster went the dancers; then, gradually, the co-ordination of their limbs began to go, their eyes glazed over, their waving arms seemed heavy and hard to control. Round and round, more and more wildly now; and beyond the firelit circle, the dark jungle out of which this hypnotic drumming was born, to which it belonged, with its primeval fears and watchful spirits.

Suddenly one of the dancers slumped to the ground while the rest continued their gyrations. I looked at the prostrate figure. His eyes were wide open but sightless, and when I spoke to him he made no response: his trance was total. The weird, monotonous throbbing went on and on, and one by one the other dancers, too, collapsed, until there was no one left. Abruptly, the music stopped. An eerie silence fell over the dancers, over the watchers, over the *ladang*, over the jungle: only in one's head, the throbbing.

Slowly the dancers came out of their trance, like people waking from a dream. The rice and fish, my part of the bargain, were brought in, and a kind of normality returned. Then the drummers took their places, and once more the throbbing, toneless rhythm started up, and the dancers circled to its insistent beat. But by then I'd had about all I could stand; I said goodnight to Mentri Awol and slipped away and turned in. In the compound I could hear it drumming on, the heartbeat of the forest. And closer to, the scuttle of the rats, trying to snuggle into the folds of my blanket. There were always two or three of them, but that night there seemed to be dozens of the brutes; the *sewang* must have excited them too. It was still thumping away when, rats or no rats, I finally fell asleep.

I got nothing useful in the way of information about the CTs out of Pangoi; he simply denied all knowledge of them. I kept on at him in the hope that eventually he would let slip something useful; I was prepared to be patient. I'd duly signalled the good news of his surrender to all concerned, including the Department of Aborigines, and among the acknowledgements was one from Pam Gouldsbury, saying she would be arriving at the fort as soon as possible. A few days later she came in by chopper and announced that she would be taking Pangoi back with her to Kuala Lumpur for interrogation.

This seemed ridiculous to me; if I couldn't get anything out of him, I was damn sure the boffins at KL would get even less. The only compensation was the comedy of trying to get him into the helicopter. For a long time he refused to have anything to do with it, and only after a great deal of persuasion, and a pantomime in which Pam Gouldsbury pretended to burst into tears, did we finally get him aboard, and he was whisked away.

As soon as he returned, he was up to his tricks. I'd been told by the department to issue him with food, which I did. However, every time he demanded more, supposedly for his starving wife and family, but I thought it more likely to be for his starving pal, Ah Ming. So I gave him his rice in cloth bags which I'd secretly marked: sure enough, a little later, when one of my patrols found and attacked a CT camp, they found a hoard of the bags, still with their contents.

The next time Pangoi came for his issue, I pointed to the bags. 'There's your rations,' I said, showing him the marks and telling them where they'd been found. He looked as guilty as hell, very different from the truculent character I'd had to put up with for so long. But he still wouldn't answer my questions; he just stood there, with downcast eyes, shuffling his feet. At that, I kicked him out of the fort, and when he did pay us a visit afterwards he always kept well clear of me. Pangoi wasn't the only one around prepared to try and pull the wool over my eyes. In the fort we had a detachment of a special force known as the 'Police Aboriginal Guard' (PAG), who were supposed to be employed on CT killing patrols - according to the Department of Aborigines. In fact, they were far more useful as guides. Left on their own, they were prone to set off with five days' rations, breathing fire and slaughter; but as soon as they were out of sight they would settle down in the nearest *ladang* for five days, enjoying the rations and the company, then return to the fort and spring a yarn about how far they had patrolled. I soon got wise to their little game and put an end to it. The department didn't approve, but we fort commanders knew a lot more about the PAGs and their little ways than they did.

I mentioned Busu Jamin, one of the tribal headmen, who had been in on the longhouse conference about Pangoi and whom I didn't trust. One day I had a visit from him and he told me that a number of CTs were regularly visiting his *ladang*, and that he was expecting them again within the next few days. It sounded genuine, so I gave him some rice and salt and sent him on his way. I didn't tell him what I intended to do about it.

Next morning I set off with a small, well-armed group for Busu's *ladang*. We took only a couple of days' rations, and some rock salt which we could trade for native food if need be - much as I disliked it. I'd been there a number of times before, but when we arrived at his longhouse and he saw me standing there, at the foot of the steps, he looked thoroughly shaken. He quickly recovered and invited me in. If anything, it was even worse than Mentri Awol's: smokier and smellier, with an even more raucous chorus of hawking and spitting. At one end, where the worst of the racket was coming from, a group of aborigines had gathered, and they beckoned me over. In the centre lay an emaciated wreck, motionless, with staring eyes, almost, I reckoned, at his last gasp. If he didn't have proper medical treatment quickly, it pretty soon would be his last.

I told Busu we should have to take him back to the fort with us when we left. Till then, we had a job to do.

I was allotted a bed space in the longhouse, and one of my own men stayed with me. We had bren and a sawn-off shotgun; and in spite of the oppressive atmosphere it was an ideal ambush position. Unlike so many I had occupied, it was out of the rain, we could brew up without worrying about giving away our position, and we had a good killing-zone. Busu did not like the idea of us killing Ah Ming and his men inside the longhouse because of the fear of the spirits, which would surely come and plague him; but I set his mind at rest by demonstrating that we could shoot them through the bamboo slats as they came up the steps. The rest of my unit were stationed in the other longhouses, so we had the whole *ladang* covered. All we had to do was wait.

Waiting, unfortunately, meant being invited to eat with Busu and the others, and I could not decently refuse. The meal consisted of the inevitable root vegetables and fish cooked in bamboo, served on a large communal leaf. But it wasn't the food I objected to as much as the company. One man in particular was suffering from the worst case of *korab* I'd ever seen; his whole body covered in scaly, flaking skin, including his skinny arms, and his gnarled fingers which darted into, and all over, the food. I knew that if I stayed there a minute longer I should be violently sick, and I made some excuse and left. Never again, I promised myself, would I share a meal with the aborigines.

I can't say I got much sleep that night either; it was too much like being in a terminal TB ward. Also, I was becoming increasingly suspicious. Busu, I was damned certain, was plotting something, but I couldn't decide what. All I could do was be extremely wary and keep my back covered.

Next morning I told Busu to carry on as normal, and after a bit his people forgot about my being there. Until, that is, I started to get something to eat. Tins, and, above all, a tin-opener, had them 'oohing' and 'ahhing' all round me; and when I heated a pan of water over a block of solid fuel, they were utterly amazed; a magic stone that made fire! Although Busu assured me that Ah Ming and some of his followers were on their way to the *ladang,* and I kept the unit on the alert all day, nothing happened. As darkness fell, I knew they wouldn't be coming, and my suspicions deepened. What was he up to?

While I sat in the fetid, smoke-filled longhouse, amid the spitting and chattering, it was as if I were outside myself, observing this strange intruder from another world, squatting among people from a time I and my people had left behind thousands of years ago. They knew nothing of firearms or helicopters, or even tins and tin-openers; a pair of scissors was strange and wonderful in their eyes. They feared the spirits of the dead and put up with sickness and disease because they had no choice.

Then the Communists came and told them that the white man was a devil who would kill and eat them, and they believed them. Now we, those same white men, had come and brought not death but medicines for their ailments, and told them that it was the Communists who were devils. These white men, who were supposed to be so evil, even came to their longhouses and shared their food and wanted to kill only the Communists. You couldn't be surprised if the aborigines were in a muddle, not knowing whom to believe.

Yet, in their own surroundings, they survived. They built their longhouses, they had fire and cooked, and with their blowpipes and poisoned arrows they could pick off a bird in a tree as surely as I could with a twelve-bore. I had been hunting with Mentri and some of his tribe and had tried to handle the seven foot blowpipe and aim it, but I found I couldn't manage it at all. With the ubiquitous bamboo they made not only blowpipes but water-carriers, cooking vessels and houses; even, in one *ladang* I visited, an aqueduct to bring water from a stream seventy five yards away.

Their logic did not work like ours; they had no written language and a limited vocabulary. Yet, as I sat there among them in the smoky dark, I remembered what I had read about them in a paper produced by the department. As a people, they are peaceable, and one tribe will rarely, if ever, fight another. All they really want is to be left alone. Finding themselves, as they were then, under pressure from the Communists on one side and Government forces on the other, they followed the only course open to them; they tried to placate both. A few aborigines, for reasons of their own, had thrown in their lot whole-heartedly with the CTs. The great majority, like Mentri Awol and Pangoi and Busu, were more concerned with keeping out of trouble than with actively assisting either side[8]. And, one had to admit, one could see their point of view: it wasn't their quarrel. But it made life difficult for poor bloody policemen like me.

My thoughts were interrupted by Rahman, the member of the patrol who was with me in the longhouse, bringing me a mug of tea.

'*Tuan* is deep in thought?' he said.

'Yes. What do you think's going on?'

'I'm not sure, *Tuan*. All the men are suspicious of Busu. Maybe he's trying to have us ambushed.'

I thought of the trap that had been laid for us by Pangoi and Ah Ming, from which we had been saved by Mentri Awol. I went to look again at the sick man. Busu was quickly at my side.

'Will you take him back to the fort?' He asked.

'Yes.'

'You're sure?'

'Of course. I said so.'

He shuffled off. I saw most of the night out watching the dancing flames from the fire making grotesque shapes about the longhouse, and wondering why Busu was so insistent that we take the sick man with us. It wasn't simply anxiety over his health, I was sure. When dawn came at last, I had made up my mind: I called Rahman.

'We'll leave in half an hour,' I said; 'tell the others to be ready'.

When Busu realised we were going, he asked me again about the man.

'Sure,' I said. 'Get him ready, and have four of your people lined up to carry him.'

'But you said *you* would take him.'

'I haven't enough men to spare. You have plenty, and he's your tribe. We will take him, but your people must carry him.'

When he saw I meant it, he started to make excuses: he hadn't enough men, they had to go hunting, and so on.

'If he doesn't get to the fort,' I said, 'he'll die.'

But there was no shifting him, and in the end we left without him. It was then, as we were padding along the track that would take us back to the fort, that I suddenly thought I saw what it was all about. Busu had got us to his *ladang* on the pretence that Ah Ming would be there. Then he tipped off Ah Ming, who would be waiting for us somewhere along the way. We would have been an ideal target, lumbered with a sick man on a stretcher. It was a guess, but it all fitted.

I halted the men and put it to them, and they all agreed. They had picked up hints of it in the longhouses; Pangoi's name had been mentioned. Far from Busu betraying Ah Ming, it seemed far more likely that Busu had been trying to set me up. That being so, I checked our position, took a compass bearing on the fort, and led them off the track. It was hard work, with a lot of climbing through thick bush, but if my deductions were correct it was the safest way. It took us a lot longer, but eventually we got back to the fort without incident. As I took a leisurely bathe in the river, and then doused myself with anti-lice powder, I thought: so that's it. It's Ah Ming or me, and so far I'm ahead on points. Let's keep it that way.

Among the signals that had come in while I'd been away was one that read: 'On the next airdrop, a supply of soap will be included, and this is to be distributed to all the aborigines on Mentri's *ladang*.' End of message. All I could do was laugh. Were they serious or taking the mickey? The aborigines had never seen a bar of soap in their lives; they'd probably eat it, or try to light a fire with it - they certainly wouldn't put it to its proper use. I could only imagine that some intrepid desk-warrior, on a visit to the fort, had been so overcome by the aboriginal pong, or, worse still, had become so infested with head and body lice - 'dancing dandruff', we called it - that he had decided the aborigines needed cleaning up.

Anyway, there it was, boxes of it stacked in my shack, so I sent for Mentri and a couple of his brighter lads and set about enlightening them on its use. Once they'd got the general idea, I packed them off with a box each, and instructions to issue one cake to each member of the *ladang* and tell them what to do with it. There was enough in the boxes, I explained, to last the *ladang* for seven days. If Mentri looked a bit puzzled, I put it down to his normal mental fog where numbers were concerned. And off he went.

Next day he was back. 'More soap, *Tuan*.'

'But you had enough for seven days,' I said. 'What are you doing with it?'

'Washing in the river, as you said. Come. I show you.'

I picked up my nine mm pistol and followed him down to his *ladang*. Yes, they'd all used the soap as instructed. But where was it now? We used it, and then threw it away. Through my laughter, I realised that they thought it only worked once: one hundred and fifty bars of soap, I calculated, had gone down the river that afternoon, all in almost mint condition. Wait till they hear of that back at HQ, I thought. I reported it with a straight face. No more soap arrived. No doubt someone would dream up another wheeze for the poor benighted fort commander to ponder over.

I'd been in the fort for over three months without a break, and so accustomed was I to the life that only when visitors dropped in did I realise how strange and spartan it must seem to them. Stuck out in the middle of nowhere with no other Europeans; washing in the river; living on fish, rice and the occasional tin of bully; picking off the lice; listening to the rats at night, and the eerie jungle noises; surrounded by these squat little people with their, to us, anti-social habits and incomprehensible gabble - yes, it was odd; and I loved it. I'd always yearned for adventure, for exotic and out-of-the-way places, and here I had a unique opportunity to live among stone-age people in a spot about as out of the way as anyone could want. If only I'd studied anthropology and had more time! What a wealth of myth, folklore and customs the Temiar possessed which I could do little more than guess at.

I knew a little about them through the work and publications of the Department of Aborigines. I knew that the Temiar were one of two groups who lived in the forests from the Perak-Kelantan border in the south to northern Selangor. Those around Fort Brooke were the Temiar-Senoi; those further south were the Semai-Senoi. They lived, as I saw for myself, partly by hunting, partly by a 'slash-and-burn' form of agriculture. Within the strictly recognised group areas, each under its own headman - Mentri, Busu, etc. - they would clear a *ladang*, plant it with crops such as tapioca, maize, gourds, tobacco, hill rice and other vegetables, cultivate it for a year, then move on. Four or five years later, they would return to the original place and start the cycle again. The Temiar were different from nearly all the other groups (the Negritos to the north on the Thai border, the aboriginal Malays to the south) in that more than one family shared a longhouse.

These things I knew, but very little more; only what I could learn from watching them, talking to them in a jumble of two languages, neither of which I knew properly, and trying to win their trust. Being the only European was an advantage in that, apart from the members of my police unit, there was no one else for me to talk to; moreover, the very nature of my job fostered a closer understanding of them.

All the same, I looked forward to the arrival of visitors - and usually looked forward to their departure before very long. One bunch who arrived on a fact-finding mission stayed longer than they intended or I wanted; for soon after their chopper landed, the weather worsened and the pilot decided it was too bad to take off. They were stuck in the fort for three days, and it was amusing to see how differently they reacted to the experience. One or two took to it quite well; the others did not. What, no electricity? Nowhere to wash? And these aborigines everywhere - how could I bear to have them around, even sitting at my table, with their revolting habits! Ugh! As civilly as I could, I explained that they were my source of information, my lifeline, and my safeguard. They were the reason I was there. I'm not sure they really understood.

One of them was a real pain. He grumbled about everything, not least when he got a leech-bite on his ankle. He made such a fuss I really enjoyed telling how I'd had them all over me, in my hair, my armpits, my crutch.

'One even got into my penis,' I said (it was perfectly true), 'I had to use a thorn with great precision and dexterity to extract it before it disappeared inside. I pissed blood for several days afterwards.'

The look on his face was worth the agony of the actual experience; I felt quite sorry for him.

'It's all right, I said, 'your little leach-bite won't go septic.'

He didn't believe me, and was very glad when there was a sudden break in the weather and they were able to leave. Once again, I was on my own and could get back to business.

eleven

goodbye to fort brooke

While the fact-finding party was around – and I daresay they found a few facts they hadn't expected – I'd had none of the snippets of information I relied on, such as movements of CTs, rumours of camps and so forth. My uninvited guests had scared the aborigines off. One afternoon not long after they'd gone, Mentri came spluttering in to see me. As he'd already been in to see me that morning, I knew it must be something important. When he'd cadged the inevitable cigarette, puffed on it several times and had a good scratch, he gave me the news – and some news it was. A tribe of aborigines who had been classed as hostile wanted sanctuary in the fort.

'Great,' I said. 'How many are there?'

Mentri produced a length of rotan and laboriously tied nine knots in it: each knot was supposed to represent ten.

'Ninety,' I said. 'I'll take food and medicine and go to them with some of your people.'

'No.' Mentri said. 'This tribe has never seen a white man. You'll frighten them away.'

I laughed. 'Perhaps they'll frighten me,' I said. 'I'm dead scared of you, you know!'

When the bantering was over, I gave him some rice, rock salt and a few cigarettes as a reward for the information, and he shuffled off, promising that they'd be at the fort in a couple of days.

I spent the next forty eight hours in some suspense. If they did come in, it would be quite a coup. Sure enough, after two days, they arrived, all ninety three of them: men, women and children. Mentri's arithmetic had been correct, near enough. I went out to greet them. As I walked amongst them, some did indeed cower away in terror, while others appeared to adopt a threatening attitude towards me. Yes, old Mentri was right, I was the first white man they'd ever seen, and some of them were scared. They were in poor shape, too; some had festering, running sores, many had the flaking skin that denoted *korab*, and all were desperately thin. Poor wretches, I thought.

Obviously, the first thing they needed was food, and I organised rice to be cooked and given to them. I handed out cigarettes to the men but not to the women; that's taboo. I had an ulterior motive, of course: I wanted to break down their fear and get on friendly terms with them because it seemed to me that they must have some knowledge of the CTs, even of Ah Ming himself. He was always in my mind; I was determined to track him down.

I asked Mentri to bring their headman and some of the elders of the tribe to my quarters where I could talk to them; but although I plied them with fags and biscuits – and scared the daylights out of them by turning on my portable radio! – I quickly saw I was going to get no information out of them. It was bloody frustrating. I had a little mascot perched by the radio, and nothing would persuade them that it wasn't this that was producing the sounds. They were truly petrified of the white man's talking *Ju-Ju*, and they fled. Nevertheless, for a couple of weeks they came daily to the fort for their rations – a special airdrop had brought extra supplies. After that, they settled down on their own *ladang* near the fort and fended for themselves.

The question in my mind was whether they had come in from the cold, of their own accord, or whether, as I suspected, they'd been sent in by the Malayan Communist Party's aborigine organisation, the ASAL. According to information issued by the Department of Aborigines, quite a number of aborigines in an area north of the fort were under Communist influence, but were wondering whether to seek the protection of the Government. It was my firm belief that my theory was the right one – after all, why else should they refuse to give any information? I was sure too that some of the food that was dished out to them found its way to Ah Ming and his CTs. At the same time, I could understand their problem. The CTs were often ruthless towards any aborigines whom they know, or suspected, had given information to the Security Forces. All I could do was feed them, as I'd been ordered, and try to persuade them that they were secure under my protection.

I'd been warned of an impending operation, code-named 'Hastings': a combined effort by police and military to try and flush out a number of CT gangs in the Fort Brooke area. My leave, which was due, was cancelled, and I was summoned to HQ at Ipoh for briefing.

Mere fort commanders didn't rate a chopper – they were for the joy-riders – so early one morning I set out with a section of men on the three-day trek to 2nd Police Field Force HQ. There, at least, were old friends whom I hadn't seen for months, and hot baths and cold beer – a pleasant change. At the briefing we were told that as a preliminary to the ground operations the RAF was going to bomb the area. This always seemed to me a complete waste of time, unless it was preceded by the placing of devices known by the code name of 'loadstone'. These were specially adapted radios which were secretly placed so that they would be discovered by CT gangs. To all appearances they were normal radios; but they not only received normal broadcasts, they transmitted a signal on which aircraft could home in on. A great deal of clandestine work had to be done beforehand for 'loadstone' to succeed, but for 'Hastings' the crude and ineffective carpet-bombing of the jungle had been planned. To my mind, it was like dropping bombs in the sea in the hope of hitting a passing submarine. Not for a mere police lieutenant to reason why. Fort Brooke was going to be in the centre of operations anyway, so I should be kept on my toes for a bit.

I was all set for the plod back when I heard that a new chopper crew, fresh out from the UK, needed flight experience over jungle, so I suggested they fly me with some much-needed supplies. The pilot agreed; my stores were loaded aboard, and off we went, pilot, co-pilot, and me. It was a lovely bright day, and there shouldn't have been any trouble finding Fort Brooke. It lay east of Ipoh, mostly over mountainous country. The landmarks were two peaks, Gunong Korbu which was 7,000 feet, and Gunong Raya which was 6,000 feet. They lay approximately half-way between Ipoh and the fort, and pilots had told me that the best route to the fort from Ipoh was to make for the two peaks, fly between them, then carry on east. It sounded a straightforward enough route in clear weather.

As we flew along over the endless green carpet of jungle, I imagined the feelings of a patrol, maybe lost and hungry, struggling through it. They would hear the chopper, and , like castaways seeing a ship, would think salvation was a hand. Then I thought of their dismay as it went clattering on its way. I must have been preoccupied with these thoughts, for it was only at that moment that I started to pay attention to the ground below – and got a nasty shock. Where were the two mountains? And the rugged country between them and the fort? This was flat jungle, nothing like the territory we should have been over; and according to my watch, we should have been there by now.

The crew had reached the same conclusion. We were lost, and fuel was running low. Did I know where we were?

'I reckon we're well to the south of the fort,' I said.

'I'll have to land soon,' the pilot said. 'If I see a clearing, I'll drop into it. We're almost out of gas.'

'Hang on as long as you can,' I said. I went to the open doorway and scanned the endless, unbroken sea of green. Not a break, not a clearing. If we crash-landed in the trees, we'd be lucky to get away with it, and I would have to find our way out of the jungle. With increasing desperation, jammed in the doorway, I searched the forest below; and, for a second, caught a glint of light. The sun reflecting off a river or a waterfall? Then I lost it. I shouted to the pilot and pointed, and he swung the machine in that direction. I stared and stared and couldn't pick it up again.

Ahead of us was a ridge. The pilot lifted the machine over it, and then I saw it again, that bright glint of light. The crew had seen it too. A minute later, there were buildings, a DZ, a landing ground.

'It's Fort Telanok,' I yelled. 'We're OK!'

Police Lieutenant Chapman, the Fort Commander, whom I hadn't seen since my days in Kuantan, came out to welcome us.

'What's all this, then? Paying surprise calls in a chopper, eh? It's all right for some!'

Somewhat shamefacedly, the pilot explained. He'd decided to follow the rivers that were clearly marked on his map, without realising that often they're screened by the dense forest for miles. Some rivers you can't see at all unless you're right over the top of them, and often not even then if the trees overhang them. He'd learnt his first lesson in flying over jungle and he was lucky – so was I. He'd only had a few minutes fuel left – and the tin roof I'd glimpsed had only been there for a few days.

'In fact,' Chapman remarked, 'the blokes hate it; it's too bloody hot under it.'

'Never mind that,' I said. '*Atap* doesn't reflect the sun, tin does.'

After a welcome drink – both for us and the machine – we set off again, heading north over the mountainous jungle country, dodging the odd peak, and this time landed safely at Fort Brooke. We off-loaded the stores, replaced them with the salvaged parachutes from the airdrops, gave the lads a conducted tour of the premises (during which Mentri appeared and relieved them of their cigarettes), and off they went – wiser but not, luckily for them, sadder. Maybe, I thought, there's a case for doing the journey on foot, after all.

'Operation Hastings' was upon us: a stream of wireless messages, choppers coming and going, for the fort was at the centre of things.

S51s, loaded with men and equipment, thumped down and, after heavy rain, dug great trenches in the LZ with their wheels. These had to be filled in, and I had a couple of aborigines as a working party, to do the job. On one occasion, when I was called away to answer a call on the VHF, the aborigines pissed off; and a little Sycamore managed to touch down with one wheel in the ruts and very nearly went arse-over–tip. I witnessed the episode. The rotor blades were within inches of the ground when the pilot realised what was happening and took off again. So much for helicopters, I thought.

The flap didn't last long and didn't achieve anything, and life at the fort slipped back into its old routine, with a bit of variety thrown in. I mentioned earlier that I'd been on a hunting expedition with the aborigines, and this was when it took place, after the traffic generated by 'Operation Hastings' was over. One day I saw Mentri and several of his tribe setting out with their blowpipes, and asked if I, and a couple of my chaps, could join them. They agreed cheerfully, and off we went.

The hill Temiars' blowpipes are made of bamboo and are about seven feet long. They are beautifully made and decorated, and each man has his own, with which he can, literally, hit the ace of spades on a playing card at twenty paces just as well as the gun-slingers of the wild west with their six-shooters. The poison on the tip of the darts is made from the sap of the Ipoh tree, boiled until it is a dark, treacly liquid. Its effect is to paralyse the heart. If a dart pierces a vein, a man will die within a minute or two; if it doesn't enter a vein, death may take up to half an hour. Either way, it's effective enough and there isn't an antidote. Unlike modern weapons, the 'charge' is human breath, though the dart cannot be recovered and used again, as the tip breaks off. The poison doesn't affect the prey as food.

However, there is one snag – you've got to hit what you're aiming at, and this was where I was lacking. The Temiar youths learn young and soon become expert; but you try stalking some small bird or *tupai* through the forest, then raising the unwieldy blowpipe to your lips, aiming it and giving a great puff to send the dart on its way. It's not easy, I assure you, and on this particular expedition even the experts only managed to bag one small bird.

Bamboo must be about the most useful plant in creation. Apart from blowpipes and vessels for carrying water, you can eat the young shoot, use it to build houses and lie trenches, and make *panjis* – the deadly spikes sticking eighteen inches out of the ground at forty five degrees used as a defence. We had these as a belt, four to five yards wide, girdling the fort, and laced with barbed wire. I once tried working my way through this obstacle: after two feet I gave up, with nasty wounds in my hand and ankle – wounds which inevitably turned septic. They were treated with an aborigine poultice made of things it was better not to ask about. But it worked: the cuts healed cleanly within a matter of days.

Malayan weather goes in for extremes, and in a series of storms early in 1955 we had days of continuous heavy rain accompanied by winds of hurricane force. The winds ripped the *atap* roofs off a couple of the buildings, and the rain turned the river into a raging, swollen torrent in which tree trunks were swept along and crashed into our flimsy swingbridge. With no first-class information coming in regarding Ah Ming or other CT units, I was able to put repairs in hand.

For five days during this spell of storms, the fort was cloaked in mist and our regular airdrops had to be called off. Several times the aircraft flew and I could hear them rumbling low overhead, but our only contact was by radio; it was far too thick for them to attempt a drop. Food was running low and I had to introduce careful rationing. Luckily, there were no guests in the fort; no idle mouths to feed, no grumblers to listen to.

Eventually the weather cleared a bit. I got on to Ipoh on the radio and that afternoon the aircraft appeared through a break in the clouds, and the twenty nine brightly coloured parachutes came floating down. What a sense of relief, until I searched the packs for the six inch nails I'd requested for rebuilding the fort and found some wag had changed the order to one inch nails. What did they think I was doing – building a doll's house? What's more, the meat they'd sent was crawling with maggots and stank: it must have been sitting loaded in the heat for the whole five days. The river level had dropped, so I thought, 'If the boneheads at HQ can't supply us with fresh food, I'll provide it myself.' There was some plastic explosive in the fort, and, accompanied by some of the men and watched by a wondering crowd of aborigines, I blasted the river so thoroughly it nearly altered its course. The result – enough lovely large fish for everyone, including Mentri and his tribe. The explosive scared them, and when they saw the stunned fish they couldn't believe their eyes.

'It would take me all my life to catch so many,' Mentri said, and did his utmost to scrounge some of the explosive off me.

Not long after this, the official mail contained a memo: 'Arrange food and accommodation for combat platoon under Police Inspector Chan, arriving fort within four or five days.'

Chan? Chan! – surely not the man who had deserted me on that operation in Johore, the man whose religion forbade him to take life, the man who had a headache? I remember vividly the hard words I'd used. If it was the same man, the meeting was going to be pretty uncomfortable for the both of us. No, I decided, Chan would never have been put in charge of a combat platoon; he was probably keeping an office chair warm somewhere.

Four days later, one of the aborigines reported the approach of 'many armed people.' I questioned him, and it seemed that this was indeed the expected platoon, but I could see no sign of them. How did the aborigines manage to get this information to me hours before the platoon's arrival? The speed and efficiency of their 'jungle telegraph' never ceased to amaze me. That evening the guard reported that the patrol was at the swingbridge, and I alerted the bren-gun section that commanded the bridge until positive identification was established – you couldn't be too careful.

It was them all right. They had had a gruelling march over the mountains and were pretty exhausted, though I couldn't help noticing that their leader seemed brisk enough as they struggled up the steep slope to the fort. He even went back to help a straggler who was on his last legs. I watched this little drama with interest. When the platoon commander had finally got his men into the fort he came up to me and shook me firmly by the hand. I recognised him instantly. This was him, all right, the one and only Chan from Johore.

'Welcome to Brooke,' I said.

'Glad to see you again, Roy,' he said. 'Let me dismiss the platoon and I'll join you.'

Well, wonders never cease, I thought. There was a confidence about him, a panache, which I was sure was not a pose and which there'd been no sign of before. What had happened to him to cause this remarkable transformation? No doubt, I should find out; but to begin with, things were a bit strained. Neither of us quite knew whether to refer to past events or not. After supper he produced a bottle of whisky from his rucksack.

'Whisky soda, Roy?'

We both laughed, for he knew as well as I did that Fort Brooke didn't run to soda water; but somehow it broke the ice.

'I don't mind telling you,' Chan said, as we sat over our drinks in the harsh glare of the pressure paraffin lamp, with the moths and beetles crashing against the glass, 'I volunteered for this job specially to see you again and apologise. It's been on my mind ever since.'

I didn't say anything. He went on to tell me that he'd been paired with another police lieutenant, and the experience had completely changed him.

'Who was that?' I asked, and he told me. I won't mention his name, but he was known throughout Malaya as one of the toughest, meanest, and most successful jungle veterans: no wonder Chan was a changed character! He wouldn't have lasted long with this particular chap otherwise. As to our little confrontation, my suspicions that his religion had only been an excuse turned out to be false; but his experiences since had convinced him of the necessity of ridding the country of Communism, even if he, personally, had to override his beliefs.

'I was pretty livid with you at the time.' I said.

'I don't blame you,' Chan said. 'That was why I wanted to see you again and explain.'

'You have,' I said, 'and I accept it.' At that we solemnly shook hands and poured another drink. The incident was closed.

We sat on, talking of mutual acquaintances, the usual service gossip, and the level in the bottle steadily dropped. There'd been one police lieutenant we both knew who had decided to take out a life insurance policy. The company's agent brought the document, and the policeman signed it. The policeman then picked up his revolver, held it to his head and said jokingly, 'If this went off now, would the company pay up?' Then he pulled the trigger. The agent stood there in shocked disbelief as his latest client's blood trickled over the policy. He was dead before his signature had time to dry.

'Do you know if they paid up?' I asked.

'I never heard,' Chan said. 'They'd have to prove that he meant to kill himself, and that would be difficult.'

Whatever the outcome, it must have been the shortest interval on record between the issuing of an insurance policy and the death of the insured!

There was a great deal to talk about, and it was late when we turned in. By then the whisky bottle was empty, and in the morning we both woke up with sore heads.

I briefed Chan on the situation in my area, and told him of my suspicions about Pangoi, and my determination to get Ah Ming. 'Perhaps you'll have better luck,' I said, as he set off on a three-day ambush of one of the tracks I knew was used by the CTs' couriers. But neither then, nor on his later patrols, did he succeed in finding any of them, which was a shame; he deserved a success. After a couple of weeks of intensive work, he had to leave empty-handed.

And now my nine month stint at the fort was up. For good reason I kept the actual date of my departure secret. There was only one track I could use, and I had no intention of being ambushed by Ah Ming on my way. The night before, when the aborigines had left the camp and all was quiet, I sent a signal to 2nd Police Field Force HQ: 'Will be departing fort at first light. Please inform all units to keep clear of area.' Least of all did I want to be ambushed by our own people!

As I packed – and it didn't take long, I had so little to take – I thought back over my time at the fort, and realised how attached I'd grown to the place. It had been an experience which, in all its variety, I would remember with pleasure and a sense of gratitude that it should have come my way. I knew I would never forget it.

The first glimmer of light was in the eastern sky as I said goodbye to the garrison and set off with a section of men across the bamboo bridge for the last time. I headed for Mentri's *ladang*; I wanted to bid him farewell, but he wasn't there.

'He went before sun up,' I was told.

'D'you know where?'

'No,' they shrugged. Then a couple of them asked: 'Why are

you leaving us?'

'How do you know I'm leaving?'

No answer, just another shrug. Disappointed at not seeing Mentri, I set off up the steep slope out of the *ladang*, the aborigines trotting along behind me as if I were the Pied Piper. I hadn't gone far when I saw a figure sitting on a fallen tree. It was Mentri, with his blowpipe, laughing and spitting.

'What are you doing here?' I asked him

'Waiting for you.'

'How did you know I was leaving today?'

'I've told you before, *Tuan*, we jungle folk know these things,' he chuckled.

'What about Busu Jamin? Does *he* know?'

'Don't worry, *Tuan*. He knows, but you'll be safe.'

'And Pangoi? And Ah Ming?'

'No harm will come to you, *Tuan*, while you are in my area. You have been good to my people; we're sorry to see you leave.' And with that, he thrust his blowpipe and quiver into my hands.

'Take these, and keep them, and never forget us, the jungle folk, who watched over you.'

I tried to refuse, knowing how difficult it is for them to find the right kind of bamboo, free of nodes throughout its length, and how personal to himself is each aborigine's blowpipe. But he insisted, and I knew he was doing me a great honour.

'Thank you, Mentri,' I said, 'I will always treasure your gift.'[9]

I realised with dismay that I had absolutely nothing suitable to give him in return: all I could do was give him some tins of food and some rice out of my rucksack. He was pleased, but it was not a gift I would have given him if he hadn't taken me by surprise. We shook hands, said our farewells, and set off in opposite directions. I felt really sad at that moment – at leaving these gentle, unspoilt people who, through no wish of their own, had become involved in the political struggles of others. Whatever happened, they would be the losers.

Soon we were clear of the forbidding valley of the Sungei Rengil and pushing south towards Busu Jamin's *ladang*, which was on our route. He, of course, was waiting for us and at once offered us food. This time, at least, I could decently refuse!

'What news of Ah Ming?' I asked him. He looked sheepish.

'I haven't seen him for a long time,' he said.

I knew he was lying, but from now on Ah Ming was somebody else's problem. And so we set off again, heading into the mountains west of Gunong Swettenham and Gunong Penlope, up and down the steep, rugged forest trails, and at last arrived at the Blue Valley Estate. Here we were out of the jungle, and in a different world from that timeless world of the Temiar Senoi.

twelve

'what harry sees, harry hits'
– sometimes

Fort Brooke marked the end of my first tour of operations. I'd done three years, most of it in the jungle, and I wasn't sorry for a break. My leave, postponed by Operation Hastings, was due, and I went home for three months. While I was there I heard that I'd been awarded the Colonial Police Medal for 'Meritorious Service', in the Birthday Honours List. So my occasional tiffs with those in authority hadn't been held against me!

I enjoyed my leave, but three months was quite long enough. Strange as it may seem, my love of the country was as strong as ever, and I was glad to get back – back to the old routine of patrol and ambush; of sleeping in wet clothes with ants and leeches; of slogging up and down slippery tracks through mountains which reared up 5,000 feet; of fording fast-flowing rivers, and wading and trekking through mangrove swamps; of the Malayan rain that seems harder and wetter than rain anywhere else in the world; of being hungry, and stinking of that sweaty, decaying vegetation stench that got into your clothes and your very skin; of feeling knackered for days on end and yet never being able to switch off and relax.

It wouldn't suit everyone by any means; but if you didn't mind the discomfort, and could stand the strain, both physical and mental, it had an excitement and satisfaction that brought their own reward. You were involved in a job that needed doing, and which kept you at a high pitch of alertness and efficiency. Isn't that what most people really want out of life, and what civvy street so rarely provides? Isn't that why people go off and climb mountains and sail the oceans and do all the other daft and dangerous things they do? Finally, I liked the people I was working with: European, Chinese and Malay.

Anyway, after my leave I returned to the 4th Police Field Force in Johore, and for the next twenty two months, from October 1955 to July 1957, I was involved in a continuous series of jungle operations in the southern part of Malaya, centred on Kota Tinggi, Kluang, Yong Peng, and Pengerang. Many were uneventful – they made up the seven hundred hours of jungle-bashing they reckoned you had to put in between 'kills'. Others were far from uneventful.

Our chief target at the time was the 9th Independent Platoon of the CTs. They were strong and they were elusive, and since the start of the 'emergency' they had never suffered a major defeat. Their method was to emerge from the jungle, descend on some wretched little *Kampong*, plunder the shops of food and other supplies, and vanish. By the time the news reached us and we got to the village concerned, the 9th would have four or more hours start on us. The villagers were no help – they were too afraid of reprisals by the Communist fifth column to give us any information – and a five-day patrol in the surrounding jungle was nearly always fruitless.

But not always. Sometimes you would pick up the trail along which they'd retreated and you'd follow it, with due caution, for fear of being ambushed. It was real cat-and-mouse stuff – without it being clear who was the cat and who was the mouse. What usually happened was that, after some hours of anxious tracking, the trail would peter

166

out. We would carry on searching the jungle for as long as our rations allowed, and then return to HQ frustrated, and with little or nothing to report. A few days later, the 9th would strike again, perhaps with an ambush against a police convoy on a main road, and the same performance would begin all over again. After what I said earlier, you may well ask how I could possibly have enjoyed anything that managed to combine so clearly maximum discomfort with maximum exasperation; I suppose it was the tension of never knowing whether or not you might be lucky, that feeling in the pit of the stomach that was partly fear, partly excitement, partly anticipation.

The bane of our lives were the 'planners', the staff wallahs, many of whom had never set foot in the jungle. At planning conferences they would spread their hands over the maps and say to the assembled jungle squads or Field Force Platoons: 'Right, we will search these areas in the next five days.' Quite often, since their map-reading left a lot to be desired, to sweep and search 'these areas' would require weeks rather than days. Sometimes they made more dangerous mistakes. The following extract is from the diary I kept early in 1956:

Good information from contacts of a likely ambush position six miles from Kota Tinggi. Took five of my best chaps and left before daylight. Five hundred yards from ambush position I took over as leading scout; reckoned we had two hours to go before they showed up – if they were going to. Thirty yards short of the place, saw a figure standing in what was to be the killing-zone. Halted, carbine at the ready, safety-catch off. Thought quickly: is this a 9ᵗʰ Independent Platoon trap? Was the info planted? Has he seen me? Shall I fire or wait and see? Don't know why I hesitated. The figure started to walk towards me. He didn't move like a CT. Who is he? I shouted 'Halt!' in Malay. He stopped and raised his arms; I approached him cautiously. He was a Malay PC. A sound to my left. I swung round, ready to fire; and there were the rest of his squad, cowering in the undergrowth. I said to the sergeant:

'What are you doing here, Sergeant?'

'We were sent to ambush this position, Tuan.'

'So were we,' I said bitterly; 'and we're lucky to be alive to tell the tale.'

'Yes, Tuan, we are.'

The man I saw first had been standing up to have a pee; it was only that and some sixth sense that had made me pause before firing. That saved him – and probably quite a few others on both sides. I gave orders to call off the ambush and accompanied the patrol to the nearby *kampong* where the sergeant and his men lived with their families in the small police station compound. They made tea. I called up HQ at Kota Tinggi to request transport. I reported the balls-up, but it was hushed up.

Both lots of orders had come from HQ. This sort of thing didn't happen often, thank God; it was one of my worst nightmares.

Kota Tinggi is quite a pleasant small town, situated on the banks of the Johore River about thirty five miles north-east of Singapore.

Almost every year during the monsoon, the river rises and floods the town, sometimes to a depth of eight feet or more. The population is mainly Chinese, many of whom work on the surrounding rubber estates. Our Police Field Force camp was only about two miles away, so Kota Tinggi was useful as a place where you could get a haircut and a cold beer, but that was about all. If you wanted something a bit livelier, you had to drive the winding road to Johore Bahru and get ripped off in 'Amy's Bar'.

My particular pal was a bloke by the name of Noel Dudgeon, and we used to meet occasionally at Amy's. Noel was stationed at what had been a Japanese 'Kempei-Tai' base and was now a police mess; some people swore the place was haunted by the victims murdered there. Noel drove an Alvis coupe which was well known in those parts, and he had one of the hairiest jobs, for he commanded a platoon of the Special Operational Volunteer Force (the SOVF). He spoke fluent Cantonese and all his men were SEPs. One of their favourite ploys was to dress as Communists and, through their own agents with the CTs, arrange a meeting. This was all very well in theory, but if their agent had been 'turned' they could easily be led into an ambush instead of setting one up. Needless to say, all Noel's SOVF operations were top secret, and he rarely talked about them.[10]

We were to seal our friendship by driving back to England together in an antique jeep bought from a Chinese scrap yard outside Johore Bahru – but that's another story.

Noel was just one of a first-class bunch of blokes in the Malayan Police, and I often used to think, when we were in the mess having a beer together and yarning about operations past and to come, how lucky I was to be one of them. And for my next operation I had a couple of the toughest and best, 'Digger' Boyce and Harry Barlow. Briefing for it took place at Kota Tinggi police station, and was given by the local head of Special Branch, a man who had at one time been Churchill's personal detective. The three of us were in his office, and he handed us a photograph of an unpleasant-looking character with a pockmarked face.

'Take a good look at him. He's worked for the Communists for years, but he's recently turned police informer. Tomorrow morning at six o'clock, this cove will be driving a truck full of supplies for the CTs out along the Lee Saw mill logging track. The point of contact is two miles along that track. There he'll stop, as he always does, and he'll hand the supplies over. You three will follow the truck from a safe distance. According to the driver, there will be no more than three CTs at the rendezvous. When he sees them, he'll rev up his engine and stop. That's the signal; and after that it will be up to you. Any questions?'

'Yes.' I said. 'How do we know that he's right and there'll only be three? What about the 9th Platoon? Is there any danger of them appearing on the scene?'

'I can't guarantee anything, but the latest reports put them in the Pengerang area.'

'Do you know what weapons the CTs will be carrying?' Digger asked.

'One sten and two rifles.'

'Then I shall take my old faithful,' Harry said, meaning his carbine. 'You know the saying: 'What Harry sees, Harry hits.''

'And what's alive will not survive,' I added.

'I'll take a carbine as well,' piped up Digger.

'You crafty pair.' I said. 'That means I have to struggle with the bren – on a bloody bicycle!'

Because the sound of an engine in the early hours of the morning might alert the Min Yuen (the Communist fifth column), we'd decided to bicycle the eight miles to the logging track We were to set off at the cheerless hour of three am. I didn't sleep much. No one likes an informer, and that shifty, pockmarked face in the police identity photo (in which, admittedly, no one looks his best) kept on floating into my mind. Could he be trusted? Perhaps, after three years of dealing with other shifty characters like Busu Jamin, I was getting the copper's occupational disease – suspiciousness. We would, at all events, do well to keep our wits about us.

Three o'clock came at last. You may not have tried riding a bicycle when you're festooned with ammunition pouches and carrying a bren-gun over one shoulder, but believe me – well, believe Harry and Digger – it's good for a laugh. Or so they seemed to think. I managed without lights. I was in front, and I suddenly smelt cigarette smoke. I've mentioned before how, in the jungle, smells can give someone's position away, and to me cigarette smoke – cheap Chinese cigarettes at that – meant only one thing. I was off my bike and flat at the side of the road in a split second. Of course, the other two jokers assumed I'd fallen off and were doing themselves an injury trying to laugh silently.

'Get down, you stupid sods,' I muttered, 'unless you want to be shot at.'

They knew then that it wasn't a joke, and flung themselves down beside me.

'What's up?' Harry whispered.

'Can't you smell it? Cigarette smoke?'

They sniffed, and agreed. We lay there, weapons cocked, absolutely silent, for five, maybe ten minutes. The smell was still around. We listened intently; strained our eyes in the darkness. Nothing. Surely, if there were CTs about, they'd have thrown their fags away by now – or discovered us and opened fire?

When nothing happened, and yet the smell, that seemingly unmistakable smell, persisted, we held a whispered conference and decided to take a chance. We jumped on our bikes and pedalled like hell for the rendezvous. At the start of the logging track we dismounted, hid the bikes, and waited silently for poxy-face to turn up.

Slowly, the light seeped back into the sky. Not long to wait. In the distance, the sound of an engine. A lorry swung off the road, and as it slowed down I glimpsed the driver's face. That wasn't our man, and we let it go. A second lorry came grinding round the bend and passed us. The light was stronger now and I saw the driver clearly. It looked like poxy-face, but the headgear was wrong, so we let that go too: they were simply trucks on their lawful business to the logging camp. At last a third truck arrived, changed down and swung on to the track. Ah, that was poxy-face. I gave two short, low whistles. He glanced sideways, spotted me, and gave me a leery smile. As he set off along the logging track, we followed at a reasonable distance; slowly at first, then, as he accelerated, faster and faster, until we were running to try and keep up with him.

'Slow down, you bloody fool,' Barlow muttered. 'Slow down!' But of course the driver couldn't hear him.

The lorry disappeared round a bend in the track. We kept going, more cautiously now; had we gone the two miles? Round the bend, there was the truck drawn up, and two uniformed CTs talking to the driver, our driver. Trouble was, there was no cover, for the jungle here had been cleared. But they were in range. I rested the bren on Digger's shoulder and took careful aim. And at that moment, poxy-face moved directly into the line of fire.

'You stupid bastard!' I muttered to myself. 'Move!' Could I fire a burst between them without hitting poxy-face? Head of Special Branch wouldn't be too pleased if we picked off one of his pet informers.

'Move, damn you!' But would he hell!

Digger and Harry had summed up the problem, and slipped away into the undergrowth to try and outflank them. In a second they'd disappeared. I waited. Suddenly, the sharp crack of a carbine. The two CTs bolted for cover. I charged the lorry, the bren bucking against my body as I fired burst after burst. The next thing, there was poxy-face racing towards me, screaming. He threw himself down in front of me. Miraculously, he'd not been hit.

All was quiet. Digger and Harry emerged from the undergrowth and joined me by the lorry, now possessing two punctured tyres.

'I swear I hit one of them,' Harry said; 'maybe both.'

'I hope they die a long and lingering death,' Digger said.

'Trust an Aussie to be callous,' I said grinning.

There were bloodstains leading off into the jungle. We left poxy-face to be picked up, as arranged, by a Field Force Section, and set off into the bush. It was slow, tedious work, scrutinising every leaf for signs of blood, but we succeeded in tracking the wounded man for quite a distance. Then, just as we reckoned we were getting warm, the rain started. In a moment it was bucketing down, washing away every trace of evidence, and we made our way back to our bikes in a none too pleasant frame of mind. The man had probably taken refuge in the nearby swamp.

At HQ both the OC and the Special Branch chap were sympathetic: the operation had been a tricky one, and at least we'd winged one of the CTs. That evening in the mess, the Special Branch man produced a sketch of Harry Barlow in jungle-green uniform, armed with a carbine and two saucy-looking CTs waving and shouting at him. The caption read: 'What Harry sees, Harry hits.' It got a laugh, and cost him a round of drinks.

As a postscript, the wounded man did, in fact, die in the swamp. His companion at the pick-up surrendered many months later and reported his death.

thirteen

the trap

diary entry 8 february 1957

Dusk, twelve miles from Johore Bahru. Noel and I are encamped in jungle close to a rubber estate. This could be a very dodgy operation, as it depends on the good faith of an SEP, Chang Ah Tien, and our orders are, if possible, to capture any CTs we encounter and not, repeat not, to eliminate them. The key to it is Chang. He was a Section Leader of the 5th Independent (CT) Platoon, and was one of the ones who got away when they were surrounded by Police and Gurkhas some months ago. After that he found himself alone, with his unit split up, and well aware that he was being hunted.

It seems that at this time, when he was at a pretty low ebb, he came across a surrender leaflet, and this tipped the scales in persuading him to turn traitor. SEPs who are prepared to help the Security Forces have it pretty cushy, and the word gets around, as it's meant to. Anyway, Chang made up his mind to surrender and, being a cunning bastard, he did it secretly so that his former comrades didn't get to know of it. That way, of course, he was more valuable to us, and could hope to be rewarded accordingly. His mother lives in the village of Kulai, which is still Communist dominated, and he got her to arrange a secret RV for him with one of our senior officers. Everything went according to plan, and soon enough Chang was in Johore Bahru Police HQ with bags to eat and plenty of fags, happy as the proverbial pig in ... as they say. But he knew he was going to have to pay for the privilege, which is why Noel and I are squatting in a basha on the edge of this rubber estate and yarning about our plans to drive back to the UK from Singapore – something no one has ever done. The old jeep we've bought is almost ready, and when our six months' leave starts next February we'll be off – if we can get our visas, etc. I'm attached to Noel's SOVF just for this op, but it suits us both fine.

Going back to Chang; they fed him and debriefed him and told him what he had to do if he was to get his reward, like his old mates, Choy Lon, Hup Chuan Heng and a few others. He was to make contact with members of the 5th Platoon and lead them into an ambush – ours. He turned up this afternoon, just after we'd baled out of the truck and were padding along the track through the estate. Back at HQ they hadn't let him wash or have a haircut – his old comrades would have smelt a rat straight away if he'd come back reeking of Lux toilet soap. As he came to meet us, we knew instantly it was him – or else a genuine CT. We didn't take any chances, but it was him all right.

'On time, too' I muttered to Noel.

'Only because he wants one of my cigarettes,' Noel said, which was roughly correct. He hadn't been allowed to take any with him – it would have been another possible give-away.

Noel questioned him in fluent Cantonese and the answers Chang gave are distinctly promising. He's contacted some of his old platoon through Min Yuen coolies on the estate, and he's fixed another meeting with them tomorrow – a meeting we shall be attending as uninvited guests.

As soon as the arrangements were made for tomorrow, he disappeared back into the jungle, and we set up our camp. We've got a couple of army W/Ops, as this is army territory, and they haven't a clue. First of all, I found they were wearing boots and I told them to change into plimsolls. 'No one said anything about not wearing jungle boots,' they said, so I explained about the unmistakable print their soles make. Nobody had told them how to set up a basha either, and they made a right dog's breakfast of it – till two of Noel's chaps gave them a hand. Green as bloody grass.

9 february: tampoi barracks, johore bahru

It was a bit of a joke, really. This morning we set up our ambush. We found an ideal spot close to the camp, a clump of thick ferns overlooking the track along which Chang was to lead his victims. We staged a dummy run and then settled down to wait. It was stinking hot and the mosquitoes were diabolical.

'Lets hope the bastard's not late,' Noel whispered.

Zero hour was 14.00 hrs, and spot on time we both heard a slight movement along the track. How many would there be? The bloke in the planning staff who'd briefed us had kindly told us that if there were more than seven we could consider ourselves entitled to shoot them; fewer than seven, and we were expected to bring them back alive. Privately, Noel and I decided that three was the most we could hope to capture. We waited, safety-catches off. The sound came closer. Out we sprang, all ready for death or glory – to see one, small, ragged CT, looking, as we flew at him and disarmed

*him, extremely bewildered. The last thing he was looking for was a
fight.*

*So we radioed the news back to HQ, and they sent a car for
us. Then the three of us, Noel, I and the CT – code name Jack –
were whisked off back to the officers' mess where the beer's cool
and more than welcome. The brigadier seemed pleased enough
with our captured minnow, and wants us to go back and catch some
more. Some people are never satisfied! We've a few hours before
transport's laid on to take us back, so I think we'll nip down to
Amy's for a few beers and a bite to eat.*

10 february: police hq, johore bahuru

*Our filthy jungle-greens raised a few eyebrows in Amy's last night
– including hers – and a couple of bull-necked MPs looked at us a
bit oddly. Anybody'd think Amy's was the Ritz; though, as I said to
Noel, this is the way all ops should be conducted. 'Agreed,' he
said. 'And it works.' It worked again today.*

*This time we arranged with Chang to set our trap in a different
spot, by a stream which flowed past not far from the camp. We were
well concealed, close to the bank, with a good field of view. Along
comes Chang, followed this time by a young girl. She was in a
brand-new uniform, her hair was cropped, and she was carrying a
rifle but in a way that suggested she wasn't too familiar with it.
Opposite our ambush position, Chang waded across the stream.
For a few moments the girl was out of my view, and something hit
me on the shoulder. My God, I thought, a grenade! But it was only
her shoes. She'd taken them off to cross the stream, flung them*

over ahead of her, and scored a bull's-eye. She got the fright of her young life when, instead of her shoes, she found two desperate-looking characters who very quickly removed her rifle and informed her that she was now in British hands. Although she was absolutely terrified, she refused to talk, even though we assured her that we'd no intention of harming her – no doubt she'd been told otherwise by her leader.

Back in camp there was a nasty scene – or one that might have turned extremely nasty. We'd had to tie the girl's wrists, as we didn't want her dashing off and maybe getting shot. As she crouched there, looking first at Chang then at me, Chang said:

'She's not going to talk. Best get rid of her.' And he swung his sten in her direction. 'He's going to kill her,' Noel yelled.

I brought my carbine to within inches of Chang's chest and said, 'If you so much as touch her, I'll fire.'

He looked at me, and I said, 'Drop your gun!'

'You wouldn't shoot me,' he said.

'Try me,' I said, 'Go on, try me. I wouldn't mind saving the Government a few thousand dollars, I promise you.'

I remember suddenly noticing that everything had gone utterly still. The girl gave a slight sob, and I slipped the safety-catch.

'Chang, he's not fooling. Drop your gun,' Noel said softly.

Chang looked round. He knew we meant it. He screamed something at the girl, then slowly lowered the sten and put it down. I hadn't finished with him, though.

'Any more trouble from you,' I said, and held the carbine to his eye-socket. He got the message.

The reason why he wanted her out of the way, of course, was that she was a possible threat to him until she talked. Once she'd betrayed her comrades, as he had, they'd both be on equal terms – traitors together. The drama, such as it was, had the desired effect. After a bit, she called to Noel and me, asking us to untie her. She wouldn't try to escape, and she'd give us all the information we wanted. I daresay they'll get that out of her back at HQ; what we got this afternoon was her life-story, and fairly unusual it is. Her English is perfect, for she was in college in Singapore and got involved in the student riots last year when my platoon was placed on Red Alert. She didn't say how deeply involved she was, but the police were after her and she panicked, and fled from the city and found her way into the jungle and the arms of the CTs. Finding us waiting for her had really shaken her: at first she thought we were Russians who had come to help the Communist cause. It had taken some time for the truth to sink in. All she wants now is to wipe out the past and start afresh. I should say she's genuine; she's only 17, after all. It was noticeable how, once she'd agreed to talk, Chang's attitude towards her changed. He no longer had anything to fear from her.

Noel and I sneaked her out and brought her back to HQ. I heard just now that Chang's surrender has got back to the CTs, so that's that. We shan't be going out again tonight.

That wasn't quite the end of the story. While 'Jill', as we called her, was being rehabilitated, she was courted by one of Noel's men, Corporal Kam, who had been with us when she was captured. The affair prospered, and after a few months they got married. I was away on patrol, unfortunately. I would love to have been there; it would have completed the saga, somehow. I did see her later, though, and found it quite hard to believe it was the same person who had slung her shoes across the river and hit me on the shoulder with them. We had a good laugh about that; but there was no mistaking her relief at having escaped from the clutches of the CTs, or her gratitude at being saved from Chang's threats.

In fact, from the Security Forces' point of view too, the operation had been a success. The information supplied by Chang and the other two dealt a severe blow to the Communist organisation in South Johore, and they were forced to find new routes and build new camps. My souvenir of that operation was 'Jill's' cap with its five-pointed red star. When my own two daughters used to try it on when they were small, I would remember her capture, and the scene afterwards with Chang. As for him, I never heard of him again. With what he got paid for turning his coat, he's probably somewhere in England now, running a Chinese takeaway. If so, he's lucky. I might so easily have pulled the trigger on him that day.

fourteen

the nasty surprise department

The operation I was briefed for in March 1957 was top secret. I was to take the full platoon of thirty three men and we were to be away for twenty one days. Our destination was the area I loathed above all, Pengerang swamp, south-east of Kota Tinggi; our target was the 9th platoon – but with a difference. In my haversack I should be carrying a very special present for them.

That same afternoon I dropped in on Barlow. He was peacefully reading on his bed.

'Take a pew, Roy. What's up?'

'Have you heard? You and I are going into that lousy Pengerang swamp.'

He nodded and tossed back his long hair: his reply was typical of him.

'Good show. Hope we catch up with the 9th Platoon; that's where they're supposed to be skulking.'

That was Harry Barlow. As usual, his room looked like a miniature arsenal, a couple of hand-grenades on the dressing table, a well-oiled carbine propped up in the corner, his revolver in its jungle-green holster beside the bed.

'Some people must think we have web-feet, sending us there again,' I said.

'Seems we're to operate independently,' he said; 'you in the northern sector, me in the south.'

'I've got the orders here ...'

I was to leave at first light in a couple of days' time, and the first stage was to be by police launch. We would be carrying five days' rations, and then have to rely on air-dropped supplies. Our ground-to-air recognition signal was 'Fox One Bar', and our call sign 'Jig 5'. According to the map, it seemed that we had approximately two hundred square miles of jungle and swamp to search. After four hours by boat, we would have one or two days of difficult trekking before we reached the area. The last sentence of the orders amused me: 'All CTs encountered are to be captured or killed.' Did the Op. Planners think we'd be playing pontoon with them!

'Good luck and good hunting,' Harry said as I left.

Outside I met Sergeant Abdullah, a first-class hand just like Sergeant Shaffie. He saluted smartly and said he had been giving the platoon a lesson in map-reading.

'But it doesn't make any difference, *Tuan*. They still manage to lose themselves, don't they?'

'Don't we all, at times,' I said.

He grinned, knowing how often I'd had very little idea of our exact position; knowing, too, that we'd always succeeded in extricating ourselves eventually. During the monsoon season, rivers would appear that weren't on any map; and compass bearings, even from the tops of hills, were usually frustrated by the trees – unless one climbed them, and risked the ants!

I'd found the best way of navigating on a cross-country trek was to have a leading scout armed with a sten gun ahead of me, and to keep a constant check on his direction by compass. If he strayed, a low whistle and a hand-signal would bring him back on course. Some scouts could keep to the same bearing with very little need for correction; others were hopeless, zig-zagging all over the place. Sometimes I would lead, but not with much success: I was a zig-zagger too. Depending on the going, we rarely made more than three-quarters of a mile an hour, allowing for an occasional rest and a smoke.

'You know we're off again the day after tomorrow?' I said to Abdullah.

'Where to this time, *Tuan*?'

I told him. 'But keep it to yourself. You know how the men talk in the coffee shops.'

I didn't tell him about the 'presents' I would be carrying for the 9th platoon. That was strictly between Special Branch and myself.

From the deck of the police launch all I could see was the solid green mass of the mangrove swamp fifteen yards away on either side. The coxswain was keeping to the middle of the river; inshore, the banks were a tangle of roots, dark and slimy, and the water, the colour of mild ale, was shallow. The mist that had shrouded the Johore River when we left Kota Tinggi before dawn had cleared; now the sun was touching the tops of the trees, but we were in the dank shadow of the mangroves, and the air had the eerie swamp stench. There will be days of this ahead, I thought, as the launch nosed in towards the bank. One by one the men lowered themselves into the river and waded ashore, and I followed them. From the launch's deck, a covering party kept their weapons trained on the bank, just in case there was a reception committee waiting for us.

I felt the coldness of the water creeping up my body, and smelt the mud as my feet squelched through it towards the bank. The water was waist-deep at first, and I had my haversack, with its extra weight, perched on my shoulder. In the mud there were rotten branches and you had to place each foot carefully to avoid being tripped, as happened to several of the chaps. They and their kit would be sodden, even before the operation had begun.

As soon as we were all safely ashore, the launch reversed out into the stream, swung, and headed back to Kota Tinggi. Quickly we sorted ourselves out and checked our equipment, and Abdullah and I synchronised watches. The time was 09.45. We set off in Indian file on a compass bearing that would take us to the heart of our operational area and, we hoped, to the lair of the 9th platoon.

And heavy, filthy going it was. In some places the swamp water was merely up to your ankles, in others up to your waist. It was cool still, and deathly quiet, so quiet you could hear the laboured breath of the man behind you - until someone slipped in the glutinous ooze and went over with a splash, and everyone was suddenly doubly alert. Who knew what unseen eyes were watching as we struggled along through that airless, menacing silence.

One of the men held up two fingers in an interrogating gesture – how about a smoke? I nodded, and we stopped, slipping off packs that seemed to have doubled in weight since we left the river. I took a sip from my water-bottle. It tasted warm and brackish with the salt tablets we had to use to replace the salt lost through constant sweating. Then I borrowed a lighted cigarette to burn the leeches off my arms. As the hot end touched them, they wriggled and twisted their blood-bloated bodies before letting go. I could feel others on my ankles, but there was nothing I could do about them till I took my boots off when we bivouacked – and that wouldn't be for several hours yet.

No sooner had we stopped for a rest, it seemed, than we were off again, muscles straining under the weight of our packs, straps cutting into shoulders, sweating and cursing as the barbed and saw-toothed leaves tore at our clothes and skin. By three o'clock we were all exhausted, our progress was desperately slow, and I called a halt for the day. Two-man patrols were sent out in different directions to search for any signs of CT activity – we didn't want them on our doorsteps, thank you very much – and to look for somewhere dry to make camp.

The results were just as I'd hoped: no sign of terrorists, and a small, dry patch of jungle nearby. We moved out of the swamp and the routine of making camp got under way. One man from each section looked after the cooking while the rest built their *bashas*. Jo-Jo (yes, I was back with him again, after the interruption of Fort Brooke) made his magic with damp sticks, and soon thrust a cup of hot, grey liquid into my hand. Tea made from swamp water, with milk out of a tube like toothpaste, might not go down too well in a Lyons Corner House; it had a rather special flavour, as of long-rotted leaves and twigs, but it was drinkable, and, at the end of a long hard trek, a lot better than nothing.

What a relief, too, to ease off sodden boots, change into shorts and plimsolls, and attend to bites and scratches and the leeches that had made a meal of my legs. Then, feeling slightly more human, I strolled round and had a few words with the men. Most of them were busy cleaning their weapons. I was glad to see that the three new chaps, who only a week ago had been coppers on the beat, were settling down well, with the help of the old hands, into this rather more rugged life. They all seemed contented and in good spirits, so I went back to my own *basha*, studied the map, and worked out an approximate position. I scribbled down the map reference on the message pad and gave it to the radio operator to send. I could hear him repeating, over and over again, 'Jig 5 calling control', 'Jig 5 calling control', until, at last, he got an acknowledgement and went ahead. Back, in the Ops Room at Kota Tinggi, the green pin that represented us would be moved to its new position on the big wall map. How strange it all was, and how familiar! How familiar, yet never without the underlying tension, for somewhere in this closed and dangerous world were men whose highest aim was to take the lives of me and my platoon.

Jo-Jo brought me the jungle supper of rice and corned beef – later it would be rice and dried fish, or just rice, until the airdrop and I spooned it up hungrily. I never bothered with a knife and fork; they were just something else to carry. Fingers, as they say, were made before forks.

'Time to stand-to, *Tuan*,' Abdullah reported.

This too was routine – we did it, always, at dusk and dawn, in case of an attack. In this way, every man would know where to go and what to do and there would be less danger of panic and mistakes.

As darkness descended on the jungle, I stood the men down, and they sloped off to their *bashas*. It was still only seven pm, but no lights were to be used, so there was nothing for it but to upend my boots on sticks to foil the creepy-crawlies, sling my soaking uniform over a bush – it couldn't get any wetter, and rain might wash some of the swamp stink out of it – and settle down on my so-called bed. At first the silence was almost overpowering. Then, as if at a signal, the night noises started up: the eerie shrill of the cicadas, the staccato clicking of crickets, the deeper bass notes of frogs, a stereophonic din that would go on all night and which, after a time, you only noticed if it stopped. Then you would listen intently, wondering why.

diary entry

Two thirty am – someone was shaking my shoulder. I grabbed my carbine, but it was only one of the new lads who was on guard.

'Tuan,' he whispered, 'I can hear sounds of movements outside the camp.'

I was out of bed in a flash. It was pitch dark; the sentry was scared. I could tell.

'It is CTs?' he asked nervously.

'More likely to be an animal,' I told him. It's virtually impossible for men to move in the jungle at night.

'Over here, Tuan,' he whispered, as we picked our way through the camp.

Yes, there was something there all right. Tigers? I slipped the safety-catch off the carbine, just in case. The movement suddenly ceased. Whatever it was, it must have picked up our scent. Then, with a loud grunt, it went bounding off. A wild boar. The sentry's relief was clear in his voice.

'I'm sorry I woke you, Tuan, but...'

'You did the right thing,' I said; 'well done.' For a moment, while his nerves settled, we chatted quietly in the darkness.

'Were you scared?' I asked him. 'It's your first night in the jungle, isn't it?'

'Yes, I was.' After a moment, he asked shyly, 'Were you ever afraid, Tuan, at first?'

'Of course. I still am sometimes.'

'The men believe you are without fear, Tuan. They know your record; they tell how once you fought an armed CT and captured him and you only had a parang. Is it true?'

'Yes. It's true.'

'And you weren't scared?'

'I was shit-scared,' I said. 'If anybody tells you different, he's a fool or a liar.'

The lad calmed down. He'd be all right now. He'd admitted his fear, and now knew it was nothing to be ashamed of. I left him and crept back to my bed, where the mosquitoes decided I was fair game. With their whining in my ears and their stabbing at every exposed inch of my body, I drifted off into sleep.

The next day was murder – swamp and more swamp, and a fetid, airless heat that sets nerves and tempers at flash-point. When an iguana darted across the track just ahead of me, I jumped out of my skin. Jungle nerves catching up with me, I supposed. Keep calm, Follows! One of the men was straggling. The first time it happened, I issued him with a warning. The second time, I sent the platoon on ahead and waited for him. He looked piteous, but it was no time for softness. I grabbed him by the collar.

'Now get moving.'

'Tuan, I'm sick. I can't go on.'

I seized the gun and strode off. He just stood there, crying 'Tuan, Tuan, tolong!' (Sir, Sir, help!') I ignored him, and after a bit he came limping after me; the thought of being left alone in the jungle was more awful than keeping going. I flung his weapon at him.

'Next time, I shall shoot you.'

The threat, whether he believed it or not, worked; he gave us no more trouble.

At our first halt, one of the scouting patrols picked up a CT track, possibly the route of one of their couriers. It was not too hard to follow, for every twenty or thirty yards, saplings had been broken off or cut with a parang. We now moved with extreme caution, and I could feel the thrill of the chase stirring inside me, the big-game hunter's excitement as he picks up the lion's spoor – but we were after men.

The trail led us out of the swamp and on to dry ground. It had become more clearly defined, and I sensed that there was a camp not far away. The sweat made my eyes sting as I peered intently ahead. Then I spotted a basha, and fell flat on the ground. The others followed suit. We waited silently, listening. No sound. We crawled closer. Nobody could have heard us, or we should have known all about it.

I decided to rush it and gave Abdullah the signal. We went in, ready for a battle. It was deserted! No words could describe our disgust and disappointment, for this undoubtedly had been a 9th Platoon camp. We'd missed them by less than a week, I guessed. Bugger!

The camp had *bashas* for thirty or forty people, and had obviously been well and truly occupied. There was a stream nearby, and they had even put up a woven screen for the women – one of the lads found a brassiere, amid much merriment. There were empty tins and animal bones lying about, so they'd obviously been living well: the question was, did they intend to come back? Whether they did or not, it would suit us to stay there for a time. We could arrange an airdrop and use it as a base from which to patrol. It was also, I thought, the ideal place to leave their 'presents', for, sooner or later, they were sure to return and find them.

It's time I described the nature of this 'surprise' which had been weighing down my pack ever since we left Kota Tinggi.[11] Back at base, I'd been sent for by OC Special Branch. I reported to their HQ, and was taken by a Chinese inspector into his office. From a drawer he'd produced a bandolier of ammunition, and tossed a round across to me.

'Know what it is?'

'303,' I replied without hesitation.

'Have a good look at it,' he said. I examined it closely. It looked exactly like a normal 303 round, and I said so.

'Good,' he said; 'but it isn't "normal". If you were to fire that from a rifle or a bren, the firing mechanism and the barrel would explode, and it would probably kill you, certainly wound you pretty badly.' He gave me a funny, sardonic look. 'Not exactly "British", I agree, but…'

'There's a war on,' I said.

'Yes, quite.'

He then gave me my orders. First, I wasn't to mention it to *anybody* . Second, I was to find a likely place, where the 9th platoon or some other CT unit would be sure to find it, and I was to leave it there. And with any luck they would congratulate themselves that some Security Force idiot had left his ammo behind and proceed to use it.

And this, I thought, as I lay in my *basha* that night, this was the very place. The chances of them coming back here at some point were high; they would realise that we'd occupied it, and they would have a good nose around for anything we might have left behind. It would never occur to them that there was anything out of the way about the ammunition itself. They'd be very chuffed, and one day, perhaps weeks later, they would ambush some patrol of soldiers or police, open fire – and that would be it. It would be like the radio sets of 'Lodestone' that signalled the aircraft on to their target. 'Would it happen?' I wondered, as I contemplated the best place in which to leave this sinister, un-British, top-secret gift for our sworn enemies.

There's not much more to tell of this particular operation. Our airdrop of welcome supplies duly arrived – how bloody good those Dakota pilots were! We failed to make contact with any group of CTs, and after a few days we broke camp and headed east for the coast. We had a lot of sickness: malaria, 'Rengis Tree Rash' (which is caused simply by brushing against this particular tree) and a septic foot so swollen that I had to ask for a chopper to lift the sufferer. I went down with a bout of fever myself, but just about managed to keep going.

The less said about the trek along the beach to Pengerang village the better. It was stinking hot; plodding through the soft sand was torture; and scrambling over outcrops of rock was worse. I felt awful. We ran out of water and were reduced to searching for the tree that yields a few spoonfuls, and after that, to drinking from a small, stagnant pool we found behind the beach. It was not a journey I'd care to repeat, and by the time we reached Pengerang jetty and the police launch that had come to pick us up I was all in and slept like the dead all the way back to Kota Tinggi.

At Field Force mess, there was an atmosphere of deep depression. Any qualms I might have had about the doctored ammo were soon dispelled for when I asked what was wrong, somebody said, 'Clive Harrison's been killed; ambushed by the 9th Platoon yesterday morning.'

Apparently one bullet had gone through the observation hatch of his armoured vehicle on the road a few miles outside Kota Tinggi, and that bullet had got him.

There was a postscript to this particular operation. Several weeks later, a small group of armed village police were on a routine patrol near Pauchor, when they were caught by a section of the 9th Platoon on a well-used track near the village. Obviously the Min Yuen must have tipped the CTs off, for they were lying in wait. The police walked straight into the ambush. However, when the CTs opened up, their ammunition exploded in the breech of their rifles and bren-guns. A number of terrorists were critically injured and the rest fled. The police were unharmed. When I heard the story, I thought grimly that Clive Harrison and others murdered by the 9th Platoon had been revenged. In fact, as a result of the operation, the 9th Platoon ceased to be a force to be reckoned with. The platoon's fate was finally sealed when their leader, Fun Ming, was betrayed by a letter forged by Special Branch and was put to death by orders of the Communist Johore Regional Committee.

postscript

That operation in Pengerang swamp really marked the end of my time of the 'jungle beat'. For various reasons I'd decided to apply for the job in the Marine Police which I'd turned down five years before. I was halfway through the 'doctored ammo' business when I received a wireless message telling me to report to Marine Police HQ, Johore Bahru, when I got back.

During those last two weeks I did my damnedest to locate the 'will-o'-the-wisp' 9th Independent Platoon, but everything was against us. When we found tracks, you could bet your boots the rain would come down in torrents and wash them away; and, as I've already said in the last chapter, what with that, and sickness, we had a pretty frustrating time. Once again, Fun Ming and his platoon had given us the slip. It wasn't until later I learnt that, indirectly, we were responsible for liquidating them.

There was one amusing incident, though, on that ghastly trek back along the beach. At the time, it didn't seem all that funny – more like a sick joke. As I said, we were just about all in and, worst of all, we'd run out of water. I was shuffling along the beach, racked with thirst and fever, when I caught sight of something on the sand just above the tide line. It was a bottle made of brown glass. Well, you often find bottles washed up on the shore, and I nearly ignored it. Then, through the haze of fever, my mind registered: a bottle with its cap still on, that's odd. I looked at it more closely. A Guinness bottle, with its top still on! A drink! A mirage more like: I'm delirious,

going off my rocker. But it was real enough. Dying of thirst, and a
bottle of Guinness turns up at my feet – no, it couldn't happen. Indeed
it couldn't. As soon as I picked it up, I realised that it wasn't full,
though it did have *something* in it. I prised it open. Inside was a
rolled-up piece of paper – the classic message in a bottle. 'To the
finder of this bottle,' it said, 'GREETINGS.' And so on, as the
reproduction shows.

I won't even try to describe my feelings – they were beyond
description. Anyway, I kept it, expecting at least a case of the stuff in
return – no such luck. A polite letter and a cheap teaspoon with a
harp on it – and that was all! Whoever heaved it overboard was

hardly to know the circumstances in which it would be found; but to me, then, it felt like a particularly cruel practical joke.

Anyway, I knew, as we plodded back to the jetty at Pengerang, that this would almost certainly be my last op, the end of my jungle experience. I wouldn't be sorry to have a spell of civilised life: a cool shower whenever one felt inclined; clean clothes; a comfortable, dry bed – all the things which, in ordinary life, you take for granted. I should, for a time at least, really appreciate them.

And yet, for all the hardships of life in the jungle and the tension and fear of jungle warfare, I still felt that same, inexplicable attraction that had drawn me from the start. I couldn't explain it then, and, writing about it now, many years later, I still can't. It's one of those things certain people experience, whether it's for the jungle, the sea, mountains, or deserts, I loved being at sea, but the jungle, for me, had a certain special magic.

Readers of this book, with its descriptions of leeches and mosquitoes, drenching rain and horrible food, punishing treks up and down mountains, and through bamboo and swamp, may find that magic something they cannot share. Add to a way of life very like that of the aborigines the nerve-twisting tension of padding along a CT track and hearing a movement ahead, of freezing, braced for a burst of tommy-gun fire, and then the relief on realising that that sound was only the sweet grunt of a wild pig - and it must all seem incomprehensible.

When I originally turned down the Marine Police job, I'd been looking for adventure, and I'd certainly had that. I'd experienced the special thrill of watching the enemy padding unaware into my ambush, and that wave of sensation – blood-lust? Exaltation? Call it what you like – as my finger increased its pressure on the trigger and the butt of the bren kicked against my hip and the target-figure lurched and fell. The death of another human being; the look in the eyes of Ng Aik Peng just before I'd hit him between the eyes....

Adventure. Yes, you can call it that, and in a good cause. And it's always good to learn new skills. My tracking now was equal to that of any member of the platoon, even Sergeant Shaffie's. I could build a *basha*, trap fish, and use a blowpipe – even if I couldn't hit anything with it! At Fort Brooke, I'd had contact with primitive people and learnt much of their customs and way of life. I'd learnt to survive in indescribable conditions, and find my way through some of the most difficult country imaginable. As a result of five years of living and fighting in the jungle, my senses were as keen as a jungle animal's. In a way, I suppose that's what I'd become: a highly trained, quick-thinking jungle animal, with the animal's instinct for survival. To be successful against other jungle animals like the CTs, there was no alternative.

One of my reasons for applying for the Marine Branch was that it would give Noel and me a chance to organise our overland trip from Singapore to the UK. No one had ever done the complete journey of nearly 13,000 miles, and we were determined to be the first. We had the vehicle, a Jeep, scrapped by the army and completely overhauled and fitted with extra fuel tanks with a capacity of forty gallons. Now we began to collect all we needed for the journey. The room we shared soon looked like a cross between a junk shop and a warehouse.

It's unbelievable how much you need: ropes, jerry cans, a tent, a stove, cooking utensils, sleeping bags, tools, spares, maps – there was no end to it. It looked as if we'd need a truck to accompany us, just to carry it all.

Far the most difficult part was getting visas, especially for Burma. Our application was turned down, which really upset our plans, and we were only saved by the Chief Police Officer of Johore State, Mr J.Slater, who wangled it through the Malaya-Burma Police network. Even with that help, we received it only the day before we left.

As you can imagine, Noel and I had to put up with a good deal of friendly kidding on the lines of 'They'll never get past the Coliseum' – not the one in Rome, but a rather notorious bar in Kuala Lumpur. We became known as 'the Blighty or Bust Boys', and a few other, less complimentary titles as well. Then, when we had actually taken delivery of the Jeep (JA 6178) and were driving it round in Johore Bahru, and our room began to fill up with all the bits and pieces, the mood changed. People began to realise we were serious, and several – mostly HQ types we could well do without – wanted to come with us. Politely, we refused their offers.

It was less easy, in fact impossible, to refuse a final beer (well, several, actually) with our long-standing pals and colleagues in the mess before we set off. Noel and I already had long-standing hangovers from the succession of 'final beers' we'd had on previous nights. With the help of our mates we'd loaded the Jeep till it looked like a gypsy caravan. Now, with goodbyes said to the members of the platoon and to Shaffie and Abdullah in particular – I wasn't going to leave without seeing them – it really was 'one for the road'.

'What do you think our chances are?' I asked Harry Barlow.

He took a swig of beer and turned to me with a look I knew well.

'If you two so-and-so's can't make it,' he said, ' I doubt if anyone can.'

From Harry Barlow, that amounted to a vote of confidence.

'Have another beer,' I said, 'and stop taking the mickey.'

And with that, we piled into our madly overloaded vehicle and went rattling and clattering on our way back to England.

We left Johore Bahru on 1st February 1958 and reached Dover three months later, having travelled 12.666 miles, passed through 13 countries, had 10 punctures, a cracked radiator, 5 broken springs, and more breakdowns than I care to remember. The worst was in the deserts of Iran, and we should probably still be there if we hadn't managed to reach this little mud village and found, of all unlikely people, a Greek mechanic who was able to get us back on the road.

But that, as they say, is another story, and not really part of *The Jungle Beat*. In England, I got married, and with Doris went back to Malaya and the Marine Police for a further three years. But I never went back into the jungle; that part of my life ended, as I had anticipated it would, when I plodded, more dead than alive, out of the Pengerang swamp for the last time.

notes

1. Report from Malaya, Verschoyle, 1954.
2. Memsahib
3. Even today, I do not wear anything of that nature, not even a watch. It became a phobia with me.
4. Roy Henry was subsequently made Chief of Police in Hong Kong. He is now retired.
5. Indeed, our radio packed up on this occasion and on other occasions too. If we were in deep jungle and running low on stores, this could be very serious. We did have a ground-to-air panel code with which we could make a number of simple signals by laying the symbols out on the ground – H for 'SOS, ground party lost and in need of positional fix'; H with two bars under it for 'ground party has suffered casualties and is in need of assistance' and so on – but first the aircraft had to find you, and if you'd been out of touch for several days that was often far from easy.
6. Named after the CO of 22nd Special Air Service Regt, Lieutenant Colonel Oliver Brooke, DSO, MBE, partly because of the name's similarity to that of the local aborigine settlement, Sungei Brok. It is now a medical centre and school for the Temiar.
7. Busu Jamin, I learnt later, had been implicated in the murder of the anthropologist Pat Noone during the war. I had heard rumours that this was so, but neither Busu nor any other senior aborigine would talk about it: it was taboo, a secret of the Temiar and their valley. Pat (his brother Richard was in the department in KL) had spent years in the jungle and had married a Temiar girl. In accordance with tribal custom, when he was away his 'brother' would sleep with her, something which Pat, when he found out, was extremely angry about. Worse still, the 'brother' had fallen in love with the girl, and when some time later Pat went off on a trip accompanied only by Busu and the 'brother' it seemed that they killed him, for he never returned. As for the Temiar, it was as if it had never happened: an unsolved mystery of the jungle valleys. It was because of the rumours I had heard that I was extremely wary of Busu, and weighed carefully any information that he gave me.
8. Only recently did I discover documentary evidence for what I had always suspected, a pact between Pangoi and Mentri Awol, which ensured that whichever side won, the aborigines would be all right. The pact contained the following conditions:

Pangoi would continue to support the Communists as before.

Mentri Awol would give his support to the Government.

Neither was to give any information to either side which might endanger anyone in either of the two aborigine factions.

Neither was to give any information to either side which might result in a fight between the Communists and the Security Forces (because the aborigines would be blamed).

Each faction was to warn the other if either the Communists or soldiers moved against them.

All the other aborigine communities were to remain strictly neutral and maintain that they knew nothing about anything if anyone asked them.

If, in the long run, the Communists won the war, Pangoi was to ensure the safety of Mentri Awol and his people. Similarly, if the Government won, Awol would ensure that nothing befell Pangoi and his tribe.

(*From The Communist Insurrection in Malaya* by Anthony Short, Muller: 1975.)

9. I still have Mentri's blowpipe and quiver, though I don't have a great deal of use for them in England.

10. PROJECT ABBOT: Earlier on I mentioned my pal Noel Dudgeon and the Special Operations Volunteer Force (SOVF). I knew a bit about Project Abbot, which was aimed at destroying the 7th Independent Platoon and its leader, the notorious Goh Peng Tuan, but not the full details. Recently, however, I succeeded in regaining touch with Noel, who is living in Australia, and he sent me the following account. Its not really part of my story, but it gives such a vivid insight into the workings of the Special Branch of the Security Forces that it's worth including.

The operation was planned by the Circle Special Branch Officer of Kluang, E.M (Gwyn) Davies, a large flamboyant character with a theatrical flair. He controlled the leader of the Communist supply system in the Kluang area, and the Chamek branch of the Malayan Communist Party (MCP), with the exception of one man, whom the others did not trust and dared not approach for that reason. The Chamek branch consisted of the Branch Committee Member (BCM) and his wife, and three other men. The BCM was frightened that he would be found out and demanded protection, which was how I was brought into the picture.

It was arranged that I, with my platoon sergeant and five SOVF members, all dressed as CTs, would meet up with the Chamek branch and construct a hidden base next to their jungle camp, so that we could provide back-up with our automatic weapons if anything went wrong. We had direct radio communication with Special Branch for the transmission of orders and information, and for relaying instant reports of progress.

The first thing was to eliminate the odd man out in a way which would cast no suspicion on the other branch members. Through the Communist system, a supply pick-up was arranged outside the Chamek new village; an ambush was sprung by Special Branch Officers just before dawn, and the CT was shot – I suspect by the other members of his branch, but I wasn't told the details. At the same time I was squatting in the rubber with my guys, cold and wet, about a mile away. We heard the firing – most of it in the air, I think, for effect – and then moved off to the RV on the edge of the jungle where, at dawn, we met the BCM and his three companions.

We could now make our hidden base close to theirs. We built it clear of entry and exit tracks, and CT couriers came and went without ever knowing we were there. So confident was Gwyn Davies in his system, and so efficient was it, that one day, through the Communist courier service, I received a small parcel containing a letter from my mother posted in the UK five days before! A typical Gwyn Davies gesture, but one which might well have cost us our lives. We were kept supplied by the Circle Special Branch Officer. So that no leaks could occur, he came out by night, in his own car, and we met on a rubber estate not far away.

Fixing the position of Goh Peng Tuan's camp was difficult for, being a good soldier, he was constantly moving; moreover the BCM could not read a map properly, though he could find his way about perfectly well. We had to wait for him to be summoned to a meeting with Goh Peng Tuan. When the summons came, he was given a gas-operated marker balloon which he was to release through the jungle canopy as he approached the camp.

It was realised that the BCM (code name K39) wouldn't release the balloon too close to the camp out of fear for his own safety, so a constant 'cab-rank' of Auster aircraft was kept airborne to spot it and record a six-figure grid-reference. And to make sure of hitting the camp it was planned that four map-squares would be wiped out.

The operation took place at dawn on 21 February 1956. A squadron of Lincoln bombers armed with 1,000 Ib bombs went in first, followed by Vampire jets with rockets and cannon. The attack was a complete success. Goh Peng Tuan and over a hundred of his unit were killed; and it took a company from the 1st Battalion Fiji Regiment fourteen days to locate the camp, so thorough was the devastation. The whole area was a mass of uprooted and fallen trees. Months later I found that there had been two survivors, one of whom surrendered and joined my platoon.

Goh Peng Tuan was a bloody good soldier; I think you will remember his ambush of a Fiji Company in trucks, and many other incidents. I should say that the destruction of the 7th Independent Platoon did more to break the back of the MCP in Johore than any other operation. Project Abbot, as I said earlier, was a carefully planned Special Branch project, and I was just a cog in the machine, there to provide a bit of muscle if needed.

11. As far as I know, this has never before been revealed

glossary

anjang	dog	*makan*	food
api	fire	*mata mata*	policeman
atap	type of palm used for thatching walls and roofs	*Min Yuen*	Communist intelligence organisation
babi	pig	*nasi*	rice
banya besar	very big	*nibong*	type of tree
basha	shelter of wood, bamboo or atap	*orang*	person (hence orang-utan –jungle person)
bhomo	witchdoctor	*panji*	sharpened bamboo stake used as a defensive paling
bukit	hill		
chandue	opium		
chowat	loincloth	*parang*	machete
diam	quiet	*poko*	tree
gaja	elephant	*puttee*	strip of cloth wound round the leg, as a form of gaiter
gunong	mountain		
hantu	ghost		
hujan panas	warm rain	*rokok*	smoke
hutan	jungle	*rotan*	rattan, a vine used as rope or string.
ipoh	type of poison		
ja baik	be very careful	*sewang*	a traditional aborigine dance
kampong	village		
korab	a skin disease	*sona*	there
kosang	empty	*sungei*	river
kris	scallop-edged dagger	*tolong*	help
		Tuan	Sir
ladang	clearing	*tupai*	small Malayan striped squirrel
lalang	tall, coarse grass		

Forthcoming title

Publication Date: October 2000

Four Wheels and Frontiers
Roy Follows

In this, his second book, Roy Follows unveils the extraordinary journey made in an ex-army Jeep, with his firm friend Noel Dudgeon.

Extraordinary, since this was the first, and only, overland journey from Singapore to England. Against advice from notable authorities, and covering some 13,000 miles, there were no comfort blankets on this trip. No sophisticated communication systems. No sponsorship. This was a journey of irrefutable synergy and trust.

A constantly taut thread between risk and challenge, *Four Wheels* covers some of the most adverse, geographic and political conditions known, whilst opening a poignant, amusing door, into the unpredictable nature of humanity - even a life threatening ambush is handled with wit, stealth and the calm confidence of nipping to the corner ship for a pint of milk.

Other titles from TravellersEye

Discoveries

Fever Trees of Borneo

Author		Mark Eveleigh
Editor		Gordon Medcalf
ISBN	0 953 0575 69	R.R.P £7.99

This is the story of how two Englishmen crossed the remotest heights of central Borneo, using trails no western eye had seen before, to visit Borneo's last remaining independent jungle dwellers. On the way they encounter shipwreck, malaria, amoebic dysentery, near starvation, leeches, exhaustion, enforced alcohol abuse and barbecued mouse-deer foetus.

"Mark has the kind of itchy feet which will take more than a bucket of Johnson's baby talc to cure... he has not only stared death in the face, he has poked him in the ribs and insulted his mother."

The Independent

Touching Tibet

Author		Niema Ash
Editor		Dan Hiscocks
ISBN	0 953 0575 50	R.R.P £7.99

After the Chinese invasion of 1950, Tibet remained closed to travellers until 1984. When the borders were briefly re-opened, Niema Ash was one of the few people fortunate enough to visit the country before the Chinese re-imposed their restrictions in 1987. *Touching Tibet* is a vivid, compassionate, poignant but often amusing account of a little known ancient civilisation and a unique and threatened culture.

"Excellent - Niema Ash really understands the situation facing Tibet and conveys it with remarkable perception."

Tenzin Choegyal (brother of The Dalai Lama)

Dreams

Discovery Road

Authors		Tim Garratt & Andy Brown
Editor		Dan Hiscocks
ISBN	0953 0575 34	R.R.P £7.99

Their mission and dream was to cycle around the southern hemisphere of the planet, with just two conditions. Firstly the journey must be completed within twelve months, and secondly, the cycling duo would have no support team or backup vehicle, just their determination, friendship and pedal power.

"Readers will surely find themselves reassessing their lives and be inspired to reach out and follow their own dreams."   Sir Ranulph Fiennes

Frigid Women

Authors		Sue & Victoria Riches
Editor		Gordon Medcalf
ISBN	0953 0575 26	R.R.P £7.99

In 1997 a group of twenty women set out to become the world's first all female expedition to the North Pole. Mother and daughter, Sue and Victoria Riches were amongst them. Follow the expedition's adventures in this true life epic of their struggle to reach one of Earth's most inhospitable places, suffering both physical and mental hardships in order to reach their goal, to make their dream come true.

"A fantastic celebration of adventure, friendship, courage and love. Enjoy it all you would be adventurers and dream on."   Dawn French

A Trail of Visions

Guide books tell you where to go, what to do and how to do it. A Trail of Visions shows and tells you how it feels.

Route 1: India, Sri Lanka, Thailand, Sumatra

Photographer & Author	Vicki Couchman
Editor	Dan Hiscocks
ISBN 1 871349 338	R.R.P £14.99

"A Trail of Visions tells with clarity what it is like to follow a trail, both the places you see and the people you meet."   Independent on Sunday

Route 2: Peru, Bolivia, Ecuador, Columbia

Photographer & Author	Vicki Couchman
Editor	Dan Hiscocks
ISBN 0 935 0575 0X	R.R.P £16.99

"The illustrated guide."   The Times

Heaven & Hell

An eclectic collection of anecdotal travel stories – the best from thousands of competition entries.

Travellers' Tales from Heaven & Hell

Author	Various
Editor	Dan Hiscocks
ISBN 0 953 0575 18	R.R.P £6.99

"...an inspirational experience. I couldn't wait to leave the country and encounter the next inevitable disaster."   The Independent

More Travellers' Tales from Heaven & Hell

Author	Various
Editor	Dan Hiscocks
ISBN: 1 903070 023	R.R.P £6.99

TravellersEye Club Membership

Each month we receive hundreds of enquiries from people who've read our books or entered our competitions. All of these people have one thing in common: an aching to achieve something extraordinary, outside the bounds of our everyday lives. Not everyone can undertake the more extreme challenges, but we all value learning about other people's experiences.

Membership is free because we want to unite people of similar interests. Via our website, members will be able to liase with each other about everything from the kit they've taken, to the places they've been to and the things they've done. Our authors will also be available to answer any of your questions if you're planning a trip or if you simply have a question about their books.

As well as regularly up-dating members with news about our forthcoming titles, we will also offer you the following benefits:

Free entry to author talks / signings
Direct author correspondence
Discounts off new & past titles
Free entry to TravellersEye events
Discounts on a variety of travel products & services

To register your membership, simply write or e-mail us telling us your name and address (postal and e-mail).

TravellersEye Ltd
30 St Mary's Street
Bridgnorth
Shropshire
WV16 4DW
Tel: (01746) 766447
Fax: (01746) 766665
website: www.travellerseye.com
email: books@travellerseye.com